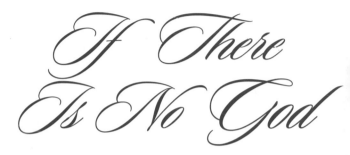

If There Is No God

Glimpses of God in Everyday Life

by
Mark Winter

RIVER
OAK
PUBLISHING

If There Is No God
Glimpses of God in Everyday Life
ISBN 1-58919-784-4
Copyright © 2001 by Mark Winter

Published by RiverOak Publishers
P. O. Box 700143
Tulsa, Oklahoma 74170-0143

Illustrations by Elise Peterson

DEDICATION

To my wife, Laura, who has revealed
God to me in so many ways.

INTRODUCTION

Every writer needs inspiration—and mine came while cooking hamburgers. As the patties sizzled on the gas grill, I sat on the back porch and admired a blazing sunset caught in the limbs of a mesquite tree. I said, to no one in particular, "If there is no God, who's painting that beautiful picture in the sky?"

Suddenly, the idea to write a book ignited in my brain. Each page would begin with the supposition, "If there is no God," then go on with a question that would kindle thoughts about God's existence, creativity, and power. I dashed into the kitchen to share the revelation with Laura, my wife. She thought it was a good idea. Then she told me to check on the hamburgers.

If there is no God, who made practical wives?

— Mark Winter

If there is no God,

who did
the math
on the cosmos?

The Milky Way blazes with more than one hundred billion stars. On the edge of the galaxy, a medium-sized star that is about 870,000 miles wide commands a solar system of nine planets. The third planet from the sun, Earth, is tilted at 23.45°—the perfect angle to support life.

Where were you when I laid the earth's foundation? Tell me, if you understand. Who marked off its dimensions? Surely you know! Who stretched a measuring line across it?

JOB 38:4-5

If there
is no
God,

?

who programmed
the most marvelous
computer of all?

What if you could own a three-pound computer that contained a hundred trillion bits of information— the equivalent of twenty million books? You already do—it's your brain.

I turned my thoughts to consider wisdom.

ECCLESIASTES 2:12

If there is no God,

who
commands the
wildflowers
to bloom?

Love flowers? So does God. In the Middle East alone, there are more than four hundred varieties of wildflowers not found anywhere else in the world.

"See how the lilies of the field grow.
They do not labor or spin.
Yet I tell you that not even Solomon
in all his splendor was dressed
like one of these."

MATTHEW 6:28-29

If there is no God,

who choreographed the waltz of the planets?

Our solar system is a ballroom where each planet dances a vast minuet around the sun. The earth alone covers about six hundred million miles every year.

The heavens declare
the glory of God;
the skies proclaim the work
of his hands.

PSALM 19:1

If there is no God,

why hasn't man
been able
to destroy the
Bible?

The French skeptic Voltaire once wrote, "If we would destroy the Christian religion, we must first of all destroy man's belief in the Bible." In 1778, fifty years after Voltaire's death, the Geneva Bible Society converted his home into a publishing firm, using his own printing press to produce thousands of Bibles. Truth is not difficult to destroy—it is impossible.

Your word, O Lord, is eternal;
it stands firm in the heavens.

PSALM 119:89

If there

is no

God,

why does the

birth of a child

fill us

with awe?

You might think that an obstetrician would get bored with childbirth. Not so with Dr. Grantly Dick-Read, who believed that the birth of a child brought the spiritual world closest to ours. In his autobiography, he observed that even irreligious mothers reported nearness to God when their children were born.

From birth I was cast upon you;
from my mother's womb
you have been my God.

PSALM 22:10

If there is no God,

why do
people pray?

Did you know that atheists and agnostics pray? According to research, nearly one in five non-professing Americans prays daily. In His kindness, God gives both hunger and food— the hunger to crave Him and the food of prayer to taste Him.

O you who hear prayer,
to you all men will come.

PSALM 65:2

If there

is no

God,

who causes the
caterpillar
to yearn for
butterfly
wings?

How does a sluggish caterpillar become a beautiful creature with stained-glass wings? In the chrysalis, the caterpillar liquefies, and new parts emerge. For a monarch butterfly, the process takes about a week. Believers in Christ also will be changed, but much quicker— "in a flash, in the twinkling of an eye" (1 Corinthians 15:52).

The Lord Jesus Christ . . . will
transform our lowly bodies
so that they will be like
his glorious body.

PHILIPPIANS 3:20-21

If there is no is no God, why do children write letters to Him?

Unlike adults, children don't need to prove the existence of God. A young boy named Charles penned this innocent profession in a letter to Heaven: "Dear God, I do not think anybody could be a better God. Well, I just want You to know, but I am not just saying that because You are God."

*"I tell you the truth, anyone
who will not receive the kingdom
of God like a little child
will never enter it."*

MARK 10:15

If there is no God,

?

who was talking
to Moses from
the burning bush?

Who spoke from the burning bush in the 1956 epic, *The Ten Commandments?* The screen credits provide no clue. Director Cecil B. DeMille, Charlton Heston, and others associated with the film have been rumored as providing the voice of God. On the other hand, the Bible boldly identifies the voice in the original burning bush as God's, and no special effects were required.

When the Lord saw that he had gone over to look, God called to him from within the bush, "Moses! Moses!" And Moses said, "Here I am."

EXODUS 3:4

If there is no God,

why is
faith
so good
for you?

In the early 1980s as a young doctor in Missouri, Harold Koenig noticed patients turning to the Bible for comfort and strength. After rigorous research, Dr. Koenig concluded that religious faith benefited ailing persons. His findings prompted him to write a book on the healing power of faith and return to his Christian roots.

"Daughter, your faith has healed you.
Go in peace and be freed
from your suffering."

MARK 5:34

If there is

no God,

who ignited the sun?

Our sun is a mid-sized model compared to the showroom of stars in the universe, yet it still packs a punch. The core, heated to an estimated twenty-seven million degrees, converts four million tons of hydrogen into energy every second. If an outside force must light a kitchen match, imagine the power of the One who ignited the sun!

In the heavens he has
pitched a tent for the sun,
which is like a bridegroom coming forth from
his pavilion, like a champion
rejoicing to run his course.

PSALM 19:4-5

If there is no God,

why have
so many
biblical
prophecies
come true?

In *Science Speaks*, Peter Stoner calculated that the probability of one person fulfilling eight selected biblical prophecies was 1 in 1,017. The likelihood of one person fulfilling forty-eight prophecies was 1 in 10,157. Jesus of Nazareth fulfilled sixty-one major Old Testament prophecies!

*Prophecy never had its origin
in the will of man,
but men spoke from God
as they were carried along
by the Holy Spirit.*

2 PETER 1:21

If there
is no
God,

who teaches
newborn whales
to swim?

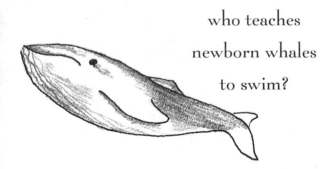

You think your child is precocious? A healthy whale calf can swim the moment it's born, rising unaided to the surface for its first breath. In one week, a baby blue whale will double in weight, eventually tipping the scales at 150 tons.

The Lord commanded the fish.

JONAH 2:10

If there is no God, who dressed penguins in their tuxedos?

With their formal-wear markings and funny waddle, penguins have become the comics of the bird world. Yet they are strictly business in the ocean, able to chase prey at speeds of up to twenty-five miles per hour.

God created . . . every winged bird according to its kind.
And God saw that it was good.

GENESIS 1:21

If there is no God,

? why has the majority
of Americans always
believed in Him?

At no point in American history have atheists outnumbered people who believe in God. In the eighteenth century, Benjamin Franklin reported that atheism was unknown in America. Today, according to research, 95 percent of Americans believe in God, while nearly 75 percent believe that all the miracles of the Bible took place.

Blessed is the nation
whose God is the Lord.

PSALM 33:12

If there
is no
God,

?

why is
the Bible
the all-time
best-seller?

A phenomenally successful modern-day author might sell two million books in a single year. In contrast, people around the world quietly purchase an estimated forty-four million Bibles every year.

So the word of God spread.

ACTS 6:7

If there
is no
God,

who causes
the body to
heal?

"Take two jokes and call me in the morning." Lee Berk, head of a research team at Loma Linda University in California, has discovered that laughter may indeed be the best medicine. A hearty chuckle can boost the immune system, decrease stress hormones, and lower blood pressure.

*A cheerful heart
is good medicine.*

PROVERBS 17:22

If there is no God,

? how did a rustic carpenter change the world?

Recognize the names Theudas, Dositheus, or Bar Cochba? Probably not. They were Jews of the early Christian era who claimed to be the Messiah. Two thousand years later, Jesus Christ—the one Christians call the true Messiah—commands an estimated two billion followers around the globe. Not bad for a small-town carpenter!

"Where did this man get this wisdom and these miraculous powers?" they asked. "Isn't this the carpenter's son?"

MATTHEW 13:54-55

If there is no God,

who told the
bumblebee
it could fly?

With their fat bodies and stubby wings, some say that bumblebees shouldn't be able to fly. But they do anyway—forward, backward, and even sideways.

"All things are possible with God."

MARK 10:27

If there

is no

God,

who put
the "pop"
into
popcorn?

Do you believe there are poltergeists in your popcorn? Native American myths told of spirits who angrily exploded from the kernels when threatened by fire. Scientists later discovered that each kernel contains moisture that expands when heated.

Then God said,
"Let the land produce vegetation: seed-bearing
plants and trees
on the land that bear fruit
with seed in it, according to their
various kinds." And it was so.

GENESIS 1:11

If there

is no

God,

why does
America pause
every year to
give thanks?

Abraham Lincoln established the national holiday of Thanksgiving in 1863, but not without some prodding from Sarah J. Hale whose editorials and letters helped institute the holiday. If you don't recognize Hale's name, you know one of her nursery rhymes—"Mary Had a Little Lamb."

?

*We give thanks to you, O God,
we give thanks,
for your Name is near; men tell
of your wonderful deeds.*

PSALM 75:1

*If there
is no
God,*

how did the

cross become a

symbol of

power?

A picture is worth a thousand words, and Christian workers in China are proving it. Armed with simple posters of the cross, they tramp into illiterate villages to explain the atonement. One elderly woman has led many people to Christ using the poster, which she carries in her bag wherever she goes.

The message of the cross
is foolishness to those
who are perishing, but to us
who are being saved
it is the power of God.

1 CORINTHIANS 1:18

If there is no God,

who sketched
pictures in
the night sky?

Betelgeuse is the Goliath of stars, forming the shoulder of Orion the Hunter. The largest known star in the sky, Betelgeuse could warehouse sixty-four million of our suns.

He is the Maker of
the Bear and Orion,
the Pleiades and the
constellations of the south.

JOB 9:9

If there is

no God,

who invented

the idea

of love?

Bertrand Russell, the Nobel Prize-winning freethinker, was an opponent of Christianity. Yet he once admitted that "Christian charity, emanating from the concept of a God of love" is the "only hope" for human survival.

We love because he first loved us.

1 JOHN 4:19

If there is no God, how did a desert tribe become a mighty nation?

Mark Twain wrote, "All things are mortal but the Jew, all other forces pass, but he remains. What is the secret of his immortality?" The answer preceded Twain by about four thousand years, when God made a promise to Abraham that He would make him the father of many nations.

*I will make your offspring
like the dust of the earth,
so that if anyone could count
the dust, then your offspring
could be counted.*

GENESIS 13:16

If there is no God,

who crammed all the data into DNA?

DNA is the stuff of genes, which determines everything from your hair color to height to resistance to certain diseases. If the coded DNA instructions within one of your cells could be printed, the information would fill a thousand encyclopedia-sized books.

I praise you because
I am fearfully and
wonderfully made;
your works are wonderful,
I know that full well.

PSALM 139:14

If there is no God,

who filled
the inkwell
of the octopus?

Be thankful for ballpoint pens. Ancient Romans wrote with a mixture of octopus ink and soot.

How many are your works,
O Lord! . . . There is the sea,
vast and spacious,
teeming with creatures
beyond number—living
things both large and small.

PSALM 104:24-25

If there is no God, who wired our nervous system?

The fastest drag racers can accelerate from zero to 280 miles an hour in less than six seconds. Some nerve impulses can zip through the human body at nearly the same speed, traveling their course in mere milliseconds.

We are God's workmanship.

EPHESIANS 2:10

If there is no God,

? who uses the sky as a canvas when the sun goes down?

Light is made of color. When the sun sets, short wavelength blues and greens bounce off dust and water particles in the air. The result? The longer wavelength colors—oranges, reds, and yellows—get through the atmosphere, creating fiery sunsets that make you want to write a poem.

My name will be great among the nations, from the rising to the setting of the sun.

MALACHI 1:11

If there is no God,

who sculpted

the mountains?

Usually we think of mountains as surface features. But huge mountains tower above the ocean floor too. The Mid-Atlantic Range stretches around several continents and ends up in the Pacific Ocean—a distance of forty thousand miles.

In his hand are the depths
of the earth, and the
mountain peaks belong to him.
The sea is his, for he made it,
and his hands formed the dry land.

PSALM 95:4-5

If there is no God,

?

who gave
flying fish
a pilot's license?

It's a bird . . . it's a plane . . . it's Super Mahi! Using their pectoral fins, flying fish can glide great distances out of water, sometimes covering the length of three to four football fields.

*God created the great creatures
of the sea and every living
and moving thing with
which the water teems,
according to their kinds.*

• GENESIS 1:21

If there is no God,

who coordinated nature's color scheme?

Green leaves actually contain various colors. In the fall, the green pigment called chlorophyll fades in the dying leaves, bringing out the fiery autumn hues that were present all along. Even in death, God can provide beauty.

*I dry up the green tree
and make the dry tree flourish.
I the Lord have spoken,
and I will do it.*

EZEKIEL 17:24

If there is no God,

who trained eagles to
care for their
nestlings?

Eagles don't have to apply for home-expansion loans. The largest nest ever found measured twenty feet deep and ten feet wide and weighed as much as a full-grown rhinoceros.

*Does the eagle soar
at your command
and build his nest on high?*

JOB 39:27

If there is no God,

who shapes the
clouds into funny
pictures?

Sky watchers have mistaken lenticular clouds for UFOs. Formed by strong winds flowing over mountain crests, these strange masses resemble towering flying saucers or mounds of fluffy pancakes.

*Do you know how God
controls the clouds and makes
his lightning flash?
Do you know how the clouds
hang poised, those wonders of him who is perfect in knowledge?*

JOB 37:15-16

If there is no God,

where do
blessings
come from?

In the great hymn, "Now Thank We All Our God," Martin Rinkart praised the Lord for "countless gifts of love." Rinkart, a seventeenth-century German priest, wrote the song in the swirling turmoil of the Thirty Years' War, soon after his wife died of pestilence.

He has shown kindness
by giving you rain from heaven
and crops in their seasons;
he provides you with plenty of food and fills
your hearts with joy.

ACTS 14:17

If there is no God,

? what is the antidote for evil?

The Tookeni tribe in Indonesia had never heard the gospel of Jesus Christ until Mission Aviation Fellowship visited them. Subsequent missions yielded the conversion of a tribal chief named Yegi Ibemi. Admitting that he had killed many people, the born-again chief said, "This is sin, and we want to follow Jesus."

Anyone who does what is good
is from God.
Anyone who does what is evil
has not seen God.

3 JOHN 1:11

If there is no God,

why do people find hope in the midst of suffering?

In 1984, journalist Terry Anderson went back to church after a long absence. Six months later, he was taken hostage in Lebanon, where he languished in prison for nine years. Anderson called his return to his Christian roots "providential," using the time to scour the Bible more than fifty times.

*Rejoice that you participate
in the sufferings of Christ,
so that you may be overjoyed
when his glory is revealed.*

1 PETER 4:13

If there is no God,

why have
many atheists
converted?

William Murray, son of atheist Madalyn Murray O'Hair, helped remove prayer from American public schools in 1963. After years of addiction and unbelief, the younger O'Hair had a dream on January 25, 1980, directing him to seek truth in the Scriptures. After a late-night search for a Bible, Murray read the Gospel of Luke and invited Christ into his life.

?

*Now in Christ Jesus
you who once were far away
have been brought near
through the blood of Christ.*

EPHESIANS 2:13

If there is no God,

who installed
Christmas lights in
the firefly?

There are more than two thousand kinds of fireflies in the world. Scientists believe that the male of each species has its own unique flashing sequence to attract a mate—which means he never has to attend a romance workshop.

Every good and perfect gift
is from above,
coming down from
the Father of the heavenly lights,
who does not change
like shifting shadows.

JAMES 1:17

If there is no God,

?

why is it human
to err and
divine to forgive?

It's not unusual for a pastor to conduct a wedding, but how many have administered vows to their son's murderer? The Reverend Walter H. Everett did just that in 1994, when he conducted the wedding of Mike Carlucci, who killed Everett's son in an argument seven years earlier. "I have accepted God's strength to forgive," Everett said.

Forgive as the Lord forgave you.
COLOSSIANS 3:13

If there is no God,

who turns the

acorn into an

oak?

Oak trees are late bloomers. Though they do not start producing acorns until they are about fifty years old, a mature oak can generate more than fifty thousand acorns in a single year.

They will be called
oaks of righteousness,
a planting of the Lord
for the display of his splendor.

ISAIAH 61:3

If there is no God,

who's answering all those prayers?

In early 1904, a young Welshman named Evan Roberts began to pray fervently for a spiritual awakening. Later that year, a fiery revival swept through Wales, packing church buildings, decreasing crime, and increasing productivity in the coal mines. Policemen even shut down their stations and formed choirs!

"I tell you, whatever you ask for in prayer, believe that you have received it, and it will be yours."

MARK 11:24

If there

is no

God,

why is
"revelation"
in the dictionary?

In 1945, a woman awoke at one o'clock in the morning, feeling an urgent need to pray for a hometown boy at war. "Lord, whatever danger Spencer is in," the woman prayed, "just cover him with a cloud." At the same time in Germany, the young soldier and his company scurried past enemy lines—a long, mysterious cloud masking their movement.

"This was not revealed to you by man, but by my Father in heaven."

MATTHEW 16:17

If there is no God,

how can we know right from wrong?

How long is a meter? The standard is a platinum-iridium bar in the International Bureau of Weights and Measures near Paris, France. To prevent changes due to temperature extremes, the bar is kept in a protected vault. God's Word is the unchanging standard by which right and wrong are measured.

?

The words of the Lord are flawless, like silver refined in a furnace of clay, purified seven times.

PSALM 12:6

If there

is no

God,

?

who filled up the oceans?

Water, water everywhere! The world's oceans blanket 70 percent of the earth's surface, representing a total volume of 340 quintillion gallons of water—that's 340 followed by 18 zeroes.

*He gathers the waters
of the sea into jars; he puts the deep
into storehouses.*

PSALM 33:7

If there

is no

God,

who invented the
formula for water?

A water molecule is composed of two atoms of hydrogen and one atom of oxygen. In the span of a century, a single molecule spends almost one hundred years in the ocean, about two weeks in lakes and rivers, and less than a week in the atmosphere.

The angel showed me
the river of the water of life,
as clear as crystal, flowing from the throne of
God and of the Lamb
down the middle of
the great street of the city.

REVELATION 22:1-2

If there is no God,

who dabbed

spots on

the leopard?

God loves variety, even in the leopard kingdom. The black panther is actually a leopard, but its spots are difficult to see because of its sleek, dark coat.

*Can the Ethiopian
change his skin
or the leopard its spots?*

JEREMIAH 13:23

If there is no God,

?

why have
great minds
meditated on Him?

Some people suffer from math anxiety. Johannes Kepler, the seventeenth-century astronomer who formulated laws of planetary motion, experienced math ecstasy. Kepler humbly admitted that he was "thinking God's thoughts after Him."

?

*Let me understand
the teaching of your precepts;
then I will meditate
on your wonders.*

PSALM 119:27

If there
is no
God,

why is the
Easter tomb
empty?

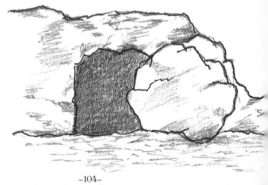

In the early twentieth century, Frank Morison set out to disprove that Jesus rebounded from the tomb. But the skeptical journalist was in for a surprise. The evidence led him to pen a brilliant defense of the resurrection called *Who Moved the Stone?*

God raised him from the dead.

<small>ACTS 13:30</small>

If there
is no
God,

who painted
the rainbow?

The colors of a rainbow are always in the same order, with red at the top and violet on the bottom. In a double rainbow, the colors are reversed.

?

Like the appearance of
a rainbow in the clouds
on a rainy day, so was
the radiance around him.
This was the appearance
of the likeness
of the glory of the Lord.

EZEKIEL 1:28

If there is no God,

? who connected the thighbone to the hipbone?

The femur is the strongest bone in the human body. It has to be. An average thighbone endures twelve thousand pounds of pressure per square inch when its owner goes for a walk.

I prophesied as I was commanded.
And as I was prophesying,
there was a noise, a rattling sound,
and the bones came together,
bone to bone.

EZEKIEL 37:7

If there is no God, why does the world celebrate Christmas?

In 1998, the Cuban government reinstated Christmas as an authorized holiday after a twenty-nine-year ban. After the announcement, Bishop Adolfo Rodriguez triumphantly announced, "The Church is separate from the state but it is not separate from the people."

For to us a child is born,
to us a son is given, and the
government will be on his shoulders. And he
will be called Wonderful Counselor, Mighty
God, Everlasting Father, Prince of Peace.

ISAIAH 9:6

If there

is no

God,

why does the world

celebrate Easter?

Members of the Russian Orthodox Church tell jokes the day after Easter. Their tradition stems from the cosmic joke that God pulled on Satan on Easter morning. Satan believed he had destroyed Christ, but God had the last laugh when He raised His Son from the dead.

With great power
the apostles continued to testify
to the resurrection of the Lord Jesus.

ACTS 4:33

If there

is no

God,

how do
we explain
that a machine
requires a maker,
but the universe
does not?

A typical wind-up alarm clock contains about a dozen moving parts. No one disputes that a skilled worker put it together. Yet some people argue that the world does not require an intelligent maker—the world that contains more than 9,000 species of birds, 70,000 kinds of trees, and 750,000 types of insects.

For by him all things were created:
things in heaven and on earth,
visible and invisible, whether thrones or
powers or rulers or authorities;
all things were created
by him and for him.

COLOSSIANS 1:16

If there is no God,

?

who installed our
blood vessels?

Imagine a distribution network that could instantly provide products to every human being on earth. Such a system exists in your body, where more than sixty thousand miles of blood vessels—enough to wrap around the earth two and a half times—transport nutrients to every cell of the body twenty-four hours a day.

The life of a creature is in the blood.

LEVITICUS 17:11

If there is no God,

who spoke to Elijah in a
still, small voice?

When Elijah heard God speak in a whisper, he probably expected a deeper voice. Ancient Jews were afraid of God's voice, which they believed could shake the earth. Indeed, the Hebrew word for "thunder" and "voice" are the same.

*After the fire
came a gentle whisper.*

1 KINGS 19:12

If there

is no

God,

who reigns over
the animal kingdom?

?

The world is a great zoo, stocked with more than a million different species of animals. They range from the elephant, the world's largest land mammal, to the pygmy shrew, which weighs about as much as a dime.

Does the hawk take flight
by your wisdom and spread his wings
toward the south?

JOB 39:26

If there
is no
God,

?

who deployed an army
in our bodies?

The Creator has equipped the average adult with about a million different antibodies, each one trained to attack a particular germ. Scientists have appropriately dubbed this army "GOD," which stands for "Generator of Diversity."

Praise the Lord, O my soul,
and forget not all his benefits—who forgives
all your sins
and heals all your diseases.

PSALM 103:2-3

If there is no God,

why do we have a
conscience?

?

In 1811, a government defrauder anonymously sent five dollars to Washington, D.C. Since then, the U.S. Treasury has managed a Conscience Fund, which has received millions of dollars from remorseful citizens.

*Our conscience testifies that
we have conducted ourselves . . . in the
holiness and sincerity
that are from God.*

2 Corinthians 1:12

If there is no God,

who sustained
the Israelites in the
desert?

For years, scholars have struggled to identify manna, the miraculous food that the wandering Israelites gathered for forty years. Some believe it was a sweet tree gum, while others speculate it was lichen that could be baked as bread. Appropriately, the word means, "What is it?"

You did not withhold your manna from their mouths, and you gave
them water for their thirst.
For forty years you sustained them
in the desert; they lacked nothing.

NEHEMIAH 9:20-21

If there
is no
God,

who spins
the world
like a top?

The earth is a heavy speedster. Weighing six sextillion tons, it can still dash through space at approximately twenty miles per second.

He spreads out the northern
skies over empty space;
he suspends the earth
over nothing.

JOB 26:7

If there

is no God,

who gets credit

for all the

outrageous

wonders in the

universe?

Years ago, a famous company advertised that its soap could float. So could Saturn, if the bathtub were large enough. Nine times bigger than earth, the ringed planet has less density than water.

How great are his signs,
how mighty his wonders!

DANIEL 4:3

If there is no God,

why have people seen angels?

Missionary John G. Paton and his wife prayed when a hostile tribe surrounded their home one night. At dawn, the tribe suddenly turned and ran. A year later, the converted chief reported that hundreds of men were standing guard at the house—huge men in radiant garments with drawn swords.

*"Do you think
I cannot call on my Father,
and he will at once put at my disposal
more than twelve legions of angels?"*

MATTHEW 26:53

If there
is no
God,

who makes
miracles?

In 1979, a young woman joined a group fleeing from Cambodia. When they couldn't find a road because of thick darkness, a swarm of fireflies appeared and lit the way. Later, the woman attended a Christian meeting and pointed to a picture of Jesus. She said, "I know that man. He is the One who led us to freedom."

?

Jesus said to them,
"I have shown you many
great miracles from the Father."

JOHN 10:32

If there is no God,

how are people
transformed?

On November 23, 1654, after a period of depression, Pascal underwent a powerful religious experience. Likening the vision to divine flame, the French scientist sewed the word "FIRE" into the lining of all his garments.

Be transformed by the renewing of your mind.

ROMANS 12:2

If there

is no

God,

why does our money

bear His name?

Everyone knows that the United States has a national anthem. But did you know that we have a national motto? The inscription on our coins and bills—"In God We Trust"—is our official national motto approved by Congress on July 30, 1956.

I will proclaim
the name of the Lord.
Oh, praise the
greatness of our God!

<small>DEUTERONOMY 32:3</small>

If there
is no
God,

?

where did
Solomon
get his wisdom?

Knowledge pays. When the Queen of Sheba visited Solomon, she was so impressed with his wisdom that she gave him 150 talents of gold, weighing more than eleven thousand pounds.

God gave Solomon wisdom
and very great insight,
and a breadth of understanding
as measureless as the sand
on the seashore.

1 Kings 4:29

If there
is no
God,

why are insects
so perfectly
engineered?

The bombardier beetle is a flamethrower on legs. When a foe attacks, it instantly mixes two chemicals inside its body and sprays the boiling vapor into the air with a loud report. The beetle itself doesn't explode because it also carries a third chemical which acts as a neutralizer in peacetime.

Let every creature praise his holy name
for ever and ever.

PSALM 145:21

If there

is no

God,

?

why have

missionaries

given up comfort?

The next time it's raining and you don't want to go to church, think about Francis Asbury. One of the first horseback missionaries of the American frontier, Asbury logged 250,000 miles in his ministry—the distance between the earth and moon.

I urge you, brothers,
in view of God's mercy, to offer
your bodies as living sacrifices,
holy and pleasing to God.

ROMANS 12:1

If there is no God,

who enrolled
the bee
in dancing
lessons?

When a worker bee finds a nectar-filled flower, it buzzes back to the hive and dances a jig. The path of the dance points directly to the flower, while another movement tells fellow workers how far away the flower is. So far, scientists have not found a dance-instructor bee.

Eat honey, my son, for it is good;
honey from the comb
is sweet to your taste.

PROVERBS 24:13

If there

is no

God,

who taught

ants

the work

ethic?

The next time you need to move your piano, think about the Formica japonica ant. It can drag an object twenty-five times heavier than its body mass, and it doesn't need casters.

Go to the ant, you sluggard; consider its ways and be wise! It has no commander, no overseer or ruler, yet it stores its provisions in summer and gathers its food at harvest.

PROVERBS 6:6-8

If there is no God,

?

what's the point?

When problems mounted for Ted Schmitt, senior vice president of Home Entertainment, he began to wonder about the meaning of life. "Is it corporate quarterly profits or something more?" he asked. Schmitt is now studying for the priesthood.

Man is a mere phantom
as he goes to and fro: He bustles about, but
only in vain; he heaps up wealth, not
knowing who will get it. But now, Lord,
what do I look for?
My hope is in you.

PSALM 39:6-7

BIBLIOGRAPHY

The author would like to acknowledge the following sources from which all facts were derived:

(p. 7) Brennan Manning, *The Ragamuffin Gospel*, (Sisters, OR: Multnomah Publishing, 1990), Chapter 2, pp. 31-33.

(p. 9) Norman L. Geisler and Ron Brooks, *When Skeptics Ask* (Colorado Springs, CO: Chariot Victor Publishing, 1989), Chapter 2, p. 21.

(p. 11) Madeleine S. Miller and J. Lane Miller, *Harper's Bible Dictionary*, "Flowers" (San Francisco, CA: Harper & Row, 1973), p. 199.

(p. 13) Manning, Chapter 2, p. 32.

(p. 15) Raymond McHenry, *Something to Think About*, "Biblical Authority" (Hendrickson, MA: Hendrickson Publishers, 1998), pp. 25-26.

(p. 17) Grantly Dick-Read, M.D., *Childbirth Without Fear*, 5th Edition (New York, NY: Harper & Row, 1944), pp. 153, 296.

(p. 19) Kenneth L. Woodward, et. al., *Newsweek*, "Talking to God," January 6, 1992.

(p. 21) "Life of a Butterfly," Olbrich's Butterfly Bonanza: www.olbrich.org.

(p. 23) Compiled by Stuart Hample and Eric Marshall, illustrated by Tom Bloom, *Children's Letters to God, The New Collection* (New York, NY: Workman Publishing, 1991).

(p. 25) Trivia for *The Ten Commandments* (1956 movie): HYPERLINK http://us.imdb.com/Trivia http://us.imdb.com/Trivia ?/004 9833.

(p. 27) Usha Lee McFarling, *Fort Worth Star-Telegram*, Knight Ridder News Service, "A Leap of Faith: Leaning on Religious Beliefs Can Heal   and Science Can Prove It," April 16, 1999.

(p. 29) DK Multimedia Staff, *Eyewitness Encyclopedia of Space and the Universe,* "The Sun's Energy" (New York: Dorling Kindersley Publishing, 1996).

(p. 31) Josh McDowell, *Evidence that Demands a Verdict,* "The Messianic Prophecies," (Here's Life Publishers, 1972), p. 167.

(p. 33) *Infopedia,* "Whales" (Future Vision Multimedia, 1994).

(p. 35) Edited by World Book Encyclopedia Staff, "Penguins," (Chicago: World Book, 1999), p. 238.

(p. 37) Tim LaHaye, Wolgemuth & Hyatt, *Faith of Our Founding Fathers,* 1987, p. 31.

(p. 39) Barna Research Online, "Beliefs: General Religious" and "The Bible," www.barna.org.

(p. 41) Allen Klein, MA, CSP, "Who Says Humor Heals?" www.canceronline.com.

(p. 43) PC Study Bible, "Christs, False," *International Study Encyclopedia.*

(p. 43) *Infopedia,* "Christianity."

(p. 45) Edited by World Book Encyclopedia Staff, "Bee," p. 201.

(p. 47) "How Popcorn Pops," http://popcorn.org/epindex.htm.

(p. 49) "She Helped Give Us Thanksgiving," http://www.bestyears.com/sarah-hale.html.

(p. 51) "Straight Talk," *Good News Magazine,* September/October 1999.

(p. 53) DK Multimedia Staff, *Eyewitness Encyclopedia of Space and the Universe,* "Supergiants Fact File."

(p. 55) LectionAid, "The Greatest So on Earth," March 13, 1994, p. 41.

(p. 57) LectionAid, "One of a Kind," September 26, 1993, p. 50.

(p. 59) Rick Gore, *National Geographic,* "The Awesome Worlds Within a Cell," September 1976, p. 357.

(p. 61) *The New Book of Knowledge*, "Ink," p. 229.

(p. 63) *The New Book of Knowledge*, "Automobile Racing" (Bethel, CT: Grolier Education, 1993), p. 538.

(p. 63) "Nervous System," innerbody.com.

(p. 65) Franklyn M. Branley, *Color: From Rainbows to Lasers*, (Crowell Co., 1978), p. 34.

(p. 67) W. Wright Robinson, *Incredible Facts about the Ocean*, Vol. 2 (Minneapolis, MN: Dillon Press, 1987), p. 48.

(p. 69) "Flying Fish," www.infoplease.com.

(p. 71) Betsy Maestro, *Why Do Leaves Change Color?* (New York: HarperCollins, 1994), p. 16.

(p. 73) Merebeth Switzer, Nature's Children: Eagles (Bethel, CT: Grolier Educational, 1986), p. 33.

(p. 75) John A. Day and Vincent J. Schaefer, *Peterson First Guide to Clouds & Weather* (New York: Houghton Mifflin Co., 1991), p. 42.

(p. 77) William J. Reynolds, "History of Hymns: Words of Thanks Written in Time of Pestilence," www.umr.org/Sfhy1120.htm.

(p. 79) National & International Religion Report, March 18, 1996. Quoted on Autoillustrator Online.

(p. 81) David Aikman, *Time*, "The World Is Fresh and Bright and Beautiful," May 18, 1992.

(p. 83) "Christian Testimony of William Murray," http://www.wjmurray.com.

(p. 85) Edited by Robert D. McHenry, *The New Encyclopedia Britannica*, Vol. 4 Micropedia Ready Reference, "Firefly" (Chicago: Encyclopedia Britannica Inc., 1994), p. 791.

(p. 87) Heather Peek, Interpreter, "Witnesses," February/March 1996.

(p. 89) David Burnie, *Eyewitness Books: Trees* (New York, NY: Alfred A. Knopf), p. 14.

(p. 91) "Bending the Church to Save the World: The Welsh Revival of 1904," www.robibrad.demon.co.uk/Revival.htm

(p. 93) David Jeremiah, *Prayer—The Great Adventure* (Sisters, OR: Multnomah, 1997), pp. 59-61.

(p. 95) *The New Book of Knowledge,* "Weights and Measures," p. 110.

(p. 97) *Something to Think About,* "Isaiah 40," p. 141.

(p. 99) Pristine Blue Home Page, "Water Trivia," www.earthsciencelabs.com/funfacts

(p. 101) *Infopedia,* "Leopard."

(p. 103) Henry M. Morris, *Men of Science, Men of God* (Green Forest, AR: Master Books, 1982), p. 13.

(p. 105) Josh McDowell, *Evidence That Demands a Verdict,* Vol. 1, p. 190.

(p. 107) *The New Book of Knowledge,* "Rainbow," p. 98.

(p. 109) Linda Allison, *Blood & Guts* (New York: Little, Brown & Co., 1976), p. 21.

(p. 111) Suecia Mendez, ALC News Service, "Cuba May Authorise Christmas Celebrations," www.churchnet.org.uk/news/files3.news207.html.

(p. 113) *Something to Think About,* "Easter Humor," p. 76.

(p. 115) *New Book of Knowledge,* "Birds," p. 211 and "Insects," p. 230, and *Infopedia,* "Trees."

(p. 117) *New Book of Knowledge,* "Circulatory System," p. 304 and "Earth," p. 9.

(p. 119) W. E. Vine, et. al., *Vine's Complete Expository Dictionary* (Nashville, TN: Thomas Nelson Publishers, 1984), p. 278.

(p. 121) *World Book Encyclopedia,* "Animals," p. 469.

(p. 123) Lawrence O. Richards, *It Couldn't Just Happen* (Nashville, TN: Word Publishing, 1987), p. 139.

(p. 123) Brand & Yancey, *In His Image* (Grand Rapids, MI: Zondervan Publishing House, Judith Markham Books, 1984), p. 85.

(p. 125) Sermonillustrator.com, "Conscience," cited from Chuck Swindoll, *Quest for Character* (Grand Rapids, MI: Zondervan Publishing House, 1993).

(p. 127) PC Study Bible, *International Standard Bible Encyclopedia*, "Manna."

(p. 129) *The Ragamuffin Gospel*, Chapter 2, p. 32.

(p. 131) *World Book Encyclopedia*, "Saturn," p. 152.

(p. 133) Autoillustrator Online, "Angels," cited from Billy Graham's *Angels: God's Secret Agents*, (Nashville: Word Publishing, 1986, p. 3).

(p. 135) Edited by Michael P. Green, *Illustrations for Biblical Preaching*, "Miracle" (Ada, MI: Baker Book House, 1982) and quoted from The Recorder, September 1979, p. 25.

(p. 137) "Blaise Pascal's Confession," www.geocities.com/Athens/6939/Confession.html.

(p. 139) "In God We Trust," U.S. Mint website, http://www.usmint.gov/facts/funfacts5.cfm

(p. 141) J. I. Packer, Merrill C. Tenney & William White Jr., *Nelson's Illustrated Encyclopedia of Bible Facts*, "Money & Economics" (Nashville, TN: Thomas Nelson Publishers, 1995), p. 331.

(p. 143) "The Bombardier Beetle," http://www.abound-ingjoy.com/beetle.htm.

(p. 145) George E. Koehler, *The United Methodist Member's Handbook* (Nashville, TN: Discipleship Resources, 1993), p. 21.

(p. 147) Lawrence O. Richards, *It Couldn't Just Happen*, pp. 113-114.

(p. 149) "Small but Strong," http://ant.edb.miyakyo-u.ac.jp/INTRODUCTION/Gakken79E/Page18.html Lyric Wallwork Winik, *Parade Magazine*, "When the Call Comes Later in Life," October 17, 1999, p. 5.

ABOUT THE AUTHOR

Mark Winter is an ordained drama evangelist who describes his One Man Show Ministries as a "creative force for God." This is his first book, although his articles have appeared in numerous publications since 1978. A native of Oklahoma, Mark and his wife, Laura, have three children and live in Texas.

If There Is No God...

Who commands
the wildflowers to
bloom?

Who causes the
caterpillar to yearn
for butterfly wings?

Who choreographed
the waltz of the
planets?

Why do ~~~~~~~~~~~~~~~

From the simple to the

profound, *If There Is No*

God presents a series of

intriguing, humorous,

scientific, and heart-

tugging questions—and

answers—to help us

discover anew the

~~~~~~~~~~ty of a Creator God.

RIVER
OAK
PUBLISHING

RO-784

gift

ISBN 1-58919-784-4

0 58919 00784 9

9 781589 197848

Illustrations by Elise Peterson
Cover Design by Whisner Design Group

TOP **10**
ICELAND

DAVID LEFFMAN

DK

EYEWITNESS TRAVEL

Left **Jökulsárlón** Right **Hot pool at Hveravellir**

LONDON, NEW YORK,
MELBOURNE, MUNICH AND DELHI
www.dk.com

Reproduced by Colourscan, Singapore
Printed and bound in China by Leo Paper
Products Ltd

First American Edition, 2010

11 12 13 10 9 8 7 6 5 4 3

Published in the United States by
DK Publishing, Inc., 375 Hudson Street,
New York, New York 10014

**Copyright 2010 © Dorling
Kindersley Limited**

ISSN 1479-344X
ISBN 978 0 7566 6140 3

Within each Top 10 list in this book,
no hierarchy of quality or popularity
is implied. All 10 are, in the editor's opinion,
of roughly equal merit.

MIX
Paper from
responsible sources
FSC™ C018179

Contents

Iceland's Top 10

Left **Súðavík** Right **Seltjarnarnes golf course, Reykjavík**

Around Iceland

Streetsmart

Left **Downtown Akureyri** Right **Skogafoss waterfalls**

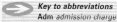

Key to abbreviations
Adm *admission charge*

3

ICELAND'S
TOP 10

ICELAND'S TOP 10

📷 Iceland's Highlights

Iceland sits on an active volcanic ridge at the edge of the Arctic Circle, its interior a wilderness of looming icecaps, solidified lava flows and black-sand deserts. Only birds and foxes inhabited the land when Scandinavian Vikings arrived in the 9th century to found the egalitarian Commonwealth of the heroic Saga Age. After 1262, when Norway and then Denmark ruled the country, Iceland fell into poverty and it was not until the 18th century that towns were established. Today, Iceland enjoys a hi-tech infrastructure and most of its 300,000 population lives around the capital, Reykjavík.

Þingvellir National Park
A broad rift valley where the European and American tectonic plates are visibly tearing apart in a riot of geology, Þingvellir National Park was the site of Iceland's Viking parliament *(see pp8–9)*.

The Blue Lagoon
Take a sauna or soak in the warm, pale blue waters of Iceland's most sublime outdoor spa, all set among a dramatic landscape of black lava boulders *(see pp10–11)*.

Geysir Hot Springs Area
Just an hour from the comforts of downtown Reykjavík, this hillside of violently bubbling pools and erupting water spouts has given its name to similar formations worldwide *(see pp12–13)*.

Gullfoss
Huge and powerful, this two-tier waterfall on River Hvítá has been a national symbol since it was saved from oblivion during the 1920s by the first environmental activist in Iceland, Sigríður Tómasdóttir *(see pp14–15)*.

Preceding pages **Gullfoss**

Lake Mývatn Area
5 Lake Mývatn collects the best of Iceland in one place: abundant wildfowl, volcano cones, mud pits, thermal pools and steaming lava flows *(see pp16–17)*.

Vatnajökull National Park
6 This colossal reserve protects not only the central Vatnajökull icecap and its score of out-running glaciers, but also a handful of exceptionally beautiful rivers, gorges and mountain formations *(see pp18–19)*.

Snæfellsjökull National Park
7 Western Iceland's long, snoutlike peninsula peaks with the snowy cone of Snæfell, a slumbering volcano crossed by hiking trails. It is tall enough to be visible from Reykjavík *(see pp20–21)*.

Látrabjarg Bird Cliffs
8 Fantastically remote even by Icelandic standards, north-westerly Látrabjarg supports one of the largest seabird colonies in Europe, and is home to millions of gulls, guillemots and puffins *(see pp22–3)*.

Landmannalaugar Area
9 Landmannalaugar's bridgeless rivers, shattered grey mountains and hot springs make you feel like an explorer in the wilds. Summer buses make this part of the Interior easily accessible *(see pp24–5)*.

Jökulsárlón
10 Make an easy tour along the Ringroad to this southeastern lagoon between the end of the glacier, Breiðamerkurjökull, and the Atlantic Ocean, full of seals and powder-blue icebergs *(see pp26–7)*.

Share your travel recommendations on **traveldk.com**

7

TOP10 Þingvellir National Park

Iceland's location on a major fault line is obvious at Þingvellir (Assembly Plains) where the land has crashed in a deep scar stretching north from Lake Þingvallavatn. In AD 930, this dramatic setting was chosen by the island's 36 chieftains as the site of their annual Alþing (General Assembly). The country's entire population of 60,000 gathered to hear the laws and to settle disputes, occasionally by combat. The Alþing's power declined after Iceland accepted Norwegian sovereignty in 1262, but the last assembly was held here in 1798.

A view of Law Rock

🏃 From the Visitor Centre, through Almannagjá, descend to the Law Rock. Take a detour to see Peningagjá and the church, then walk up to Öxarárfoss. In good weather follow hiking tracks up the rift to abandoned farms, but take care as the dense undergrowth hides deep fissures.

🍴 The only place to eat is the café at the Visitor Centre near Öxarárfoss.

- Map C5
- From Reykjavík, Golden Circle tour buses visit Þingvellir daily year-round. Some 2 and 2a buses and summer services using the Kjölur Route also stop. If driving, allow 60–90 minutes via Route 36.
- www.thingvellir.is/english
  bus: www.bsi.is

Top 10 Features

1. Lögberg (Law Rock)
2. Þingvellir Church
3. Almannagjá
4. Volcanic Features
5. Þingvallavatn
6. Flora
7. Visitor Centre
8. Wildlife
9. Öxarárfoss
10. Peningagjá

1 Lögberg (Law Rock)
A prominent outcrop below Almannagjá's cliffs, marks the site where the Alþing's Lawspeaker stood and recited the country's laws to the masses below. Look nearby for faint outlines of *buðir*, the tented camps used during Viking times.

2 Þingvellir Church
This surprisingly low-key wooden building with a black roof *(above)*, is a reminder of the Alþing of AD 1000, when, despite strong opposition from pagan priests, the Icelandic nation adopted Christianity as its sole religion. It was built in 1859 but has a 1683 pulpit.

3 Almannagjá
A walk through Almannagjá's deep, cliff-lined gully *(main image)* is a good way to appreciate Þingvellir's geology. Here, as the North American and European continental plates drift apart at 2.5 cm a year, Iceland is literally ripping in half.

4 Volcanic Features
The broad, flattened dome of northerly Skjaldbreiður – an ancient shield volcano – was the source of the lava flow now covering Þingvellir's valley. Cut by deep fissures, the lava cooled into rough a'a outcrops and pavements of smoother pahoehoe (both types of lava).

Þingvallavatn

At 84 sq km (33 sq miles) Þingvallavatn is the largest natural lake in Iceland. Its clear waters are famous for charr and trout fishing and scuba diving.

Flora

Þingvellir valley's floor is covered in a thick carpet of moss, lichen, orchids, dwarf willow and birch. Visit in autumn for exceptional colours and join locals to pick crowberries (used for jams).

Visitor Centre

Perched atop the western side of the rift on Route 36, the Visitor Centre offers superb views of Þingvellir. It also has multi-lingual films and DVDs on the region's geology and history.

Wildlife

The area just north of Þingvallavatn's lakeshore abounds in wildlife. Look for swans, mergansers and northern divers on the water and snipe, ptarmigan, mink and arctic fox on land.

Öxarárfoss

Legend has it that the falls were created when Öxará river *(left)* was diverted around AD 930 to provide drinking water during the Assemblies. During medieval times, executions were also carried out here.

Peningagjá

Peningagjá is an extraordinary sight: a narrow but deep lava fissure flooded with clear, peacock-blue water. At the bottom of this naturally-created wishing-well you can see the glinting coins.

Paying the Penalty

Lawcourts at the Alþing strangely had no power to enforce their judgements. Litigants accepted the verdicts because they reflected public opinion, but in theory – and sometimes in practice – powerful men could ignore sentences against them. The courts tried to resolve serious disputes through mediation, though the highest penalty in Viking times was not execution but being outlawed – banished from Iceland – for three years.

TOP 10 The Blue Lagoon and Around

The Blue Lagoon (Bláa Lónið) is Iceland's premier geothermal spa and one of the country's most beautiful. Set in a desolate lava wilderness, the lagoon's bright blue waters add a surreal splash of colour. You can laze in the steaming waters, have a beauty treatment, enjoy an excellent meal or stay nearby and catch the seasonal aurora display. If you have your own transport, consider a detour to see some unusual sights: Grindavík's Saltfish Museum, the Seltún hot springs and Selatangar's abandoned fishing camp.

Top 10 Features

1. Background and Origin
2. Unique Lava Setting
3. Public Bathing Pool
4. Spa Services
5. Dermatology and Health Clinics
6. Restaurant
7. Icelandic Saltfish Museum
8. Overnight Accommodation
9. Seltún Hot Springs
10. Selatangar

Shop at the Blue Lagoon

🌀 The Blue Lagoon's high mineral content can damage your hair – protect it by rubbing in conditioner before a swim and make sure you shampoo thoroughly afterwards.

☕ Apart from the main restaurant, there is a basic café at the Blue Lagoon's entrance where you can buy coffee, cold drinks and snacks.

• Map B5
• The Blue Lagoon, 240 Grindavík, 420 8800
• Several tour buses daily from Reykjavík's BSÍ station. Bus website: www.re.is
• Open 1 Sep–31 May: 10am–8pm, 1 Jun–31 Aug: 8am–9pm daily
• Adm ISK4,150
• www.bluelagoon.com
• Icelandic Saltfish Museum: Map B5
• Seltún Hot Springs: Map B5
• Selatangar: Map B5

1 Background and Origin

The Blue Lagoon was created when superheated seawater flowing out of the Svartsengi Geothermal Power Station collected in the surrounding lava *(above)*. Locals discovered that a warm dip cured skin ailments and public facilities opened here during the 1980s.

2 Unique Lava Setting

The lagoon is bordered by rough masses of black lava boulders, which lie piled high around the perimeter, hemming in the powder-blue waters.

3 Public Bathing Pool

The water at 37°C (99°F) is comfortable and the huge pool *(below)* is an amazing place to unwind with an adjacent sauna.

4 Spa Services

Enjoy a relaxing massage at the lagoon itself, or opt for a cleansing rub-down using the naturally processed fine silica, minerals, algae and salt distilled from the Blue Lagoon's waters. It is a good idea to book spa treatments in advance.

5 Dermatology and Health Clinics

The Blue Lagoon's mineral salts and white clay have long enjoyed a reputation for quickly curing eczema, psoriasis and other skin problems. You can seek specialized treatment at the Clinic *(left)* or simply buy preparations for use at home.

6 Restaurant

Enjoy fine Icelandic dishes such as grilled lobster with garlic butter, fillet of lamb or plain baked fish, with a view of the lagoon right from your table *(below)*. There is also an excellent bar accessible from the water and a café that sells wholesome snacks.

7 Icelandic Saltfish Museum

At Grindavík village, a short drive south of the lagoon is this eccentric museum that traces Iceland's fishing heritage through dioramas and photographs.

8 Overnight Accommodation

You can stay at the Blue Lagoon Clinic or the Northern Lights Inn – the latter is a fantastic spot in winter, when the colourful aurora borealis play across the night sky

9 Seltún Hot Springs

Around 22 km (13 miles) east of the Blue Lagoon, a waft of sulphur signals arrival at Seltún Hot Springs *(right)*, a geyser which blew itself apart in 1999. Stick to the boardwalk while exploring the steaming vents.

10 Selatangar

Overlooking the sea 15 km (9 miles) from the Blue Lagoon, this fishing village was abandoned in the 1850s. Ruined walls and foundations are visible through the black sand dunes and lava outcrops.

Geothermal Power

Svartsengi Geothermal Power Station takes advantage of its location over a fault line to provide cheap, green power and heating for Reykjavik. Seawater is pumped over 1 km (0.6 miles) underground, which turns to steam and is used to drive the turbines that help produce 76MW of electricity. The steam is then cooled and released into the Blue Lagoon. Five geothermal plants produce a quarter of the nation's electricity.

Geysir Hot Springs Area

The Geysir Hot Springs area lies on the lower slopes of Bjarnarfell, 90 minutes northeast of Reykjavík, and comprises a dozen or more hot water blowholes, including Geysir, the spout that gave its name to other geysers worldwide. The area became active about 1,000 years ago and today the most impressive spout is Strokkur, which you will definitely see in action. Geysir's pool is far larger but count yourself lucky if you see more than bubbles. Visit Haukadalur for an interesting old church and some undemanding hiking.

People standing beside the hot pools of Blesi

🍂 Take great care to stay on boardwalks or marked trails, and do not step into pools or their outflows, as the water is boiling hot. Falling spray from Strokkur is cool, but you will need a raincoat if you are standing downwind.

🍽 The Geysir Centre has a café serving coffee, hot dogs, drinks and sand-wiches, but the pricier hotel restaurant actually offers better value for money.

• Map C5
• The Geysir area is right by the roadside on Route 35, about 90 min from Reykjavík.
• Tour buses are available from BSÍ station Reykjavík; bus website: www.bsi.is
• Geysir hotel website: www.geysircenter.com

Top 10 Features

1. Geysir Hot Spring
2. Blesi
3. Strokkur
4. Litli Geysir
5. Konungshver
6. Haukadalur Church
7. Hótel Geysir
8. Haukadalur Forest
9. Geysir Centre
10. Bjarnarfell

1 Geysir Hot Spring
Geysir, "the Gusher", *(above)* has not erupted to its full 70-m (230-ft) height since the mid-20th century, though until the 1980s, dumping soap powder into the pool used to trigger a hiccup or two.

2 Blesi
Up the slope behind the Geysir area, Blesi, "the Blazer", is a set of twin pools, one clear and scalding; the other cooler, opaque and powder blue with dissolved minerals *(below)*.

3 Strokkur
"The Churn" *(main image)* reliably erupts every few minutes, its clear blue pool exploding in a 15–30 m- (50–100 ft-) high spout with little noise. In between eruptions, watch the water sighing and sinking as the pressure builds.

Geysir is least crowded before 10am.

Litli Geysir

Often overlooked on the walk up to Strokkur, Litli Geysir lies off the path to the left. It was probably once a water-spout that blew itself apart, and is now a small and violently slushing muddy pool, generously belching steam and bubbles.

Konungshver

Catch the "King's Spring" *(above)* on a sunny day and the colours are stunning. The clear, vivid blue water sits in a depression of orange-red rock. Get views from here of the rest of the Geysir area.

Haukadalur Church

In a woodland about 2 km (1 mile) behind Geysir, this church has a door ring said to be given to a farmer by a giant, Bergþór, whose burial mound lies nearby.

Hótel Geysir

This hotel *(above)*, right across the road from Geysir, uses the same geothermal water source to fill up its pool and outdoor hot tubs – don't miss the experience of an after-dark soak if you're here in winter.

Haukadalur Forest

Since the 1940s, Iceland's forestry service has planted millions of larches, pine and rowan trees in the Haukadalur valley. An easy walking trail passes through a gully full of waterfalls.

Geysir Centre

Directly over the road from the hot springs, the Geysir Centre has a souvenir shop *(below)*, a café and an entertaining exhibition on the history and geology of geysers. Do not miss a ride on the Earthquake Simulator.

Bjarnarfell

It is a steep hike to reach the 727 m (2,385 ft) summit of Bjarnarfell, the hill overlooking Geysir, but the rewards on a good day are spectacular views of the red-brown rock and green fields surrounding the springs.

There She Blows!

Geysers are formed in deep, vertical, flooded vents known as pipes. The water at the bottom of the pipe comes into contact with hot rock and boils, expanding upwards, while cooler water at the surface of the geyser forms a kind of lid, trapping the rising water, until so much pressure builds up that the geyser explodes skywards. Watch Strokkur and you can clearly see this lid bulging upwards just before each eruption.

⑩ Gullfoss

The powerful, two-tier waterfalls at Gullfoss on the Hvítá present a stunning sight, whether part-frozen in winter, in full flood during the spring melt, or roaring away during the long summer twilight. Their setting in a deep canyon adds to the spectacle, as does the landscape of icy peaks and gravel desert immediately north – quite a contrast to the green, spray-fed vegetation closer to the river. Take care at Gullfoss and always supervise children, as paths are slippery and there are no safety railings or warning signs.

Cafeteria at Gullfoss

🕙 Visit Gullfoss in winter to see it partly frozen and hidden under spectacular ice curtains; in summer, the afternoon provides the best lighting conditions for photographs.

🍲 Make sure you try the traditional lamb soup at the Visitor Centre café – refills are free.

• Map D4
• Daily tour buses from Reykjavík's BSÍ station; bus website: www.bsi.is

Top 10 Features

1. Origin of Names
2. Geology
3. View from the Top
4. View from Below
5. The Canyon
6. Plaque for Sigríður Tómasdóttir
7. Sigríðarstofa
8. Visitor Centre
9. Souvenir Shop
10. Kjölur

Origin of Names
Clouds of rainbow-tinged spray hanging over the cataracts have given Gullfoss its name – the Golden Falls. Hvítá (White River) is named after the light-coloured glacial sediment it carries.

Geology
The area's volcanic history can be seen on the cliffs, opposite the viewing platform, with their distinct banded ash layers from separate volcanic eruptions, overlaid with granite *(above)*.

View from the Top
The main viewing area and the safest at the falls is the platform on the top of the canyon *(main image)*. Orient yourself and take in the dramatic setting.

View from Below
Soaked by spray, you can really appreciate Gullfoss' scale from here: the river drops 10 m (33 ft), turns a right-angle and drops again *(below)*.

The Icelandic word, "foss", means "waterfall".

5 The Canyon

The canyon continues downstream from Gullfoss for 2 km (1 mile), through hexagonal basalt columns *(left)*. Follow the walking track along the top, or take a white-water rafting trip.

6 Plaque for Sigríður Tómasdóttir

A commemorative plaque to Sigríður Tómasdóttir *(left)* recalls her successful campaign to save the falls from being drowned by a dam project.

7 Sígríðarstofa

Sígríðarstofa is a local exhibition centre *(below)* showcasing the hardships of traditional life in the area, which is caught between relatively fertile plains to the west and the sterile wilderness of Iceland's frozen interior directly north.

8 Visitor Centre

The Visitor Centre at the falls includes a roomy cafeteria *(below)*, serving delicious lamb soup. The falls are invisible from here but views show mountains and glaciers.

10 Kjölur

This 160-km- (100-mile-) long route across the Interior from here runs north, traversing the grey gravel plains between the Langjökull and Hofsjökull icecaps.

9 Souvenir Shop

The souvenir shop at the Visitor Centre *(below)* has nothing specific to Gullfoss apart from postcards of the falls, but it is still a good place to find T-shirts, designer outdoor gear, books on Iceland and lava jewellery.

Saving Gullfoss

In 1907, landowner Einar Benediktsson signed away Gullfoss to be submerged by the construction of a hydroelectric dam across the river Hvítá. Sigríður Tómasdóttir, whose father was involved in the deal, was so incensed that she took legal action against the developers. Although she lost the case, public opinion ran so high in her favour that construction never began and Gullfoss was later donated to the nation as a special reserve.

🔟 Lake Mývatn Area

Known as Midge Lake in English, Mývatn's unkind label belies reality: it is a peaceful spread of water east of Akureyri, home to swarms of wildfowl in summer. The surrounding landscape, however, is anything but tranquil, with Mývatn hemmed in by a spectacular mix of extinct cinder cones and twisted lava formations, hot bathing pools, boiling mud pits and screaming volcanic vents. North-shore Reykjahlíð is Mývatn's main settlement, where you can organize tours to local sights and also to Askja Caldera in the barren Interior.

Moss campion

🌀 In summer you will need to buy face netting from local stores to protect yourself from irritating – though mostly harmless – swarms of tiny flies. They are worse on windless days.

🍽 The Gamli Bærinn restaurant-bar at Reykjahlíð has good coffee, light meals, *hverabrauð* (ryebread baked in geothermal pits) and smoked trout from the lake.

• Map F2
• Local buses and tours from Akureyri. There is an airstrip at Reykjahlíð.

Top 10 Features

1. Lake Mývatn
2. Pseudocraters
3. Dimmuborgir
4. Waterfowl Crossroads
5. Jarðböðin Nature Baths
6. Laxá
7. Krafla
8. Hverfjall
9. Askja
10. Námaskarð

Lake Mývatn
Spring-fed and covering 36 sq km (14 sq miles), Lake Mývatn was created during volcanic activity about 4,000 years ago. Lava formations *(below)* dominate the northern and eastern sides of the lake, while the rest of the shoreline is marshy.

Dimmuborgir
This weird, tumbled mass of indescribably contorted lava formations makes for an eerie hour-long wander on marked paths. Make sure you visit the drained lava tube known as Kirkja (the Church) and keep your eyes open for the rare and endangered gyrfalcons.

Pseudocraters
Looking like bonsai volcanoes, pseudocraters were formed from steam blisters popping through hot lava as it flowed over marshland. There are plenty of pseudocrater collections around Mývatn but the best, covered in grassy walking tracks, are at Skútustaðir.

Waterfowl Crossroads
Insect lava and algae in Mývatn's shallow waters provide abundant food for phalaropes, swans, divers, Slavonian grebes and 13 species of duck, including the rare Barrow's goldeneye, which breed in the lake's ice-free areas between May and August.

Bring binoculars for bird-watching.

5 Jarðböðin Nature Baths

Like the Blue Lagoon *(see pp10–11)*, Jarðböðin offers the chance to steam away in the open-air, mineral-rich geothermal waters *(left)*. The views here – west down over the lake and its volcanic setting – are even better.

6 Laxá

Laxá *(below)*, or the Salmon River, drains out of Lake Mývatn´s south-western corner and then runs to the sea near Húsavik. Walk along its banks to see harlequin duck tumbling in the rough waters between May and July.

7 Krafla

Located northeast of Mývatn, Krafla volcano last erupted during the 1720s, when its lava nearly consumed Reykjahlíð's church. Viti, Krafla's flooded crater, is bright blue *(main image)*.

8 Hverfjall

This 400-m- (1,312-ft-) high cinder cone is built from volcanic ash and gravel. A well-marked path around the crater's rim offers fantastic views.

9 Askja

South of Mývatn is Askja, an 8-km- (5-mile-) wide flooded caldera. The Víti crater nearby exploded in 1875, causing a virtual exodus of the northeast.

10 Námaskarð

Among a landscape of red clay with yellow and white streaks, Námaskarð is an area of violently bubbling, sulphurous mud pits *(below)*. Take great care as you explore.

Krafla Fires

Earthquakes between 1975 and 1984 opened up a long volcanic fis-sure at Leirhnjúkur, just west of Krafla volcano, an event that became known as the Krafla Fires. Lava poured out over the plain here, leaving behind a fascinating expanse of still-smoking formations which you can reach and explore on foot from Krafla. It is not for the faint-hearted, as the paths are rough and you need to avoid some dangerously hot spots.

Buy fishing licenses at your accommodation.

🔟 Vatnajökull National Park

Vatnajökull National Park covers 12,000 sq km (4,633 sq miles), 10 percent of Iceland's surface, and comprises the Vatnajökull icecap and disconnected areas around its fringes. The long canyons and enormous waterfalls at Jökulsárgljúfur; Skaftafell's high moorland and paired glaciers; Lónsöræfi's wilderness and remains of Lakagígar's catastrophic volcanic event can keep you occupied for days. Hiking, ice-climbing, skidooing and even dog-sledding are among the activities possible within this huge park.

Snipe in Jökulsárgljúfur

🚫 Most sections of Vatnajökull National Park are completely inaccessible in winter, closed due to bad weather or lack of buses. Plan a trip between July and mid-August to have the greatest choice of places to visit.

🍴 There are few places to eat within the park, so make sure you stock up on refreshments from the nearest town.

• Map F4
• Summer-only buses to Ásbergi and Dettifoss from Akureyri; to Skaftafell from Reykjavík and Höfn; to Lakagígar from Kirkjubæjarklaustur and Höfn. Lónsöræfi and Hvannadálshnjúkur accessible only to experienced hikers. Tours to Vatnajökull by jeep, dog-sled and skidoo from Höfn.
• www.vatnajokulsthjodgardur.is

Top 10 Features

1. Vatnajökull
2. Glacial Features
3. Hvannadálshnjúkur
4. Birdlife
5. Ásbyrgi
6. Lakagígar
7. Skaftafell National Park
8. Jökulsárgljúfur
9. Lónsöræfi
10. Dettifoss

1 Vatnajökull
Europe's largest icecap, Vatnajökull dominates the views inland from the south-west, with a dozen or more glaciers descending off its top as they slide inexorably coastwards *(below)*. At least one active volcano smoulders away underneath.

3 Hvannadálshnjúkur
Iceland's highest point at 2,199 m (7,215 ft), Hvannadálshnúkur is a *nunatak* (rocky peak) protruding from Vatnajökull's icecap. You need considerable experience to climb it. On a clear day you can see the summit from Skaftafell.

2 Glacial Features
Glaciers are slow-moving rivers of ice advancing just a few centimetres each year (though most of Iceland's glaciers are shrinking). Extreme pressure grinds down underlying rock to leave gravel morraine ridges, and squeezes out the air to give the glaciers their ice blue colour.

4 Birdlife
Sandar or deep beaches of black sand washed out from beneath Iceland's glaciers, provide nesting grounds for the greater skua, an aggressive, brown seabird which preys on weaker birds and their young.

➔ *"Jökull" means "glacier".*

Ásbyrgi
5 This gorge is believed to be an imprint of the Norse god Óðin's eight-footed horse, Sleipnir. Geologists say floods under Vatnajökull carved it *(above)*.

Lakagígar
6 This 25-km- (16-mile-) long row of craters *(main image)* was left by a devastating eruption from Kirkjubæjarklaustur in 1783. Lava and poisonous gas wiped out the farms, causing a nationwide famine.

Jökulsárgljúfur
8 The name of this national park means "Glacier River Canyon", a reference to the 120-m- (394-ft-) deep and 500-m- (1,640-ft-) wide slash through which flows Jökulsá, Iceland's second-longest river *(right)*.

Skaftafell National Park
7 This park, extending over 1,700 sq km (657 sq miles) of accessible highland plateau, offers superlative hiking along marked trails. Do not miss Svartifoss *(above)*, a waterfall framed by hexagonal granite columns, or the close-ups of blue glacier tongues streaked in gravel.

Flash Flood!
Jökulhlaups (glacial flash-floods) happen when heat from volcanos under the icecaps melts enough water to form an enclosed lake. If the lake dam gives way, the water explodes outwards with devastating results. A single prehistoric *jökulhlaup* carved out the Jökulsárglúfur canyon, while a smaller event in 1996 sent water rushing out from under Vatnajökull, sweeping away 7 km (5 miles) of the highway near Skaftafell National Park.

Lónsöræfi
9 This private reserve stretches inland from coastal lagoons through a landscape of fractured orange rhyolite mountains. It can be accessed by hiking.

Dettifoss
10 Said to be Europe's most powerful waterfall, Dettifoss *(left)* sits among a jagged grey granite landscape, its 45-m (148-ft) drop sending clouds of spray skywards. Summer-only access is along a gravel road.

Iceland's Top 10

⑩ Snæfellsjökull National Park

Established in 2001, Snæfellsjökull National Park protects the snowy snout of the Snæfellsnes Peninsula, which juts out 70 km (44 miles) into the sea from the western coast. With a beautiful conical volcano at its core, Snæfellsjökull is a place steeped in ancient, literary and New Age folklore, though most people who visit today are more interested in the mountain's hiking or climbing potential. Snæfellsjökull also makes a splendid backdrop for delving into the area's fishing history or bird-watching for rare species.

Interior of Hótel Búðir

⚑ To climb Snæfellsjökull you will need ice axes, crampons and weatherproof gear. Talk to the National Park officers at Hellissandur and Hellnar Visitor Centre about your route and weather conditions.

🍴 Hellissandur's Svörtuloft restaurant serves good pizzas.

• Map A4
• Snæfellsjökull National Park's main office: Klettsbúð 7, Hellissandur; 436 6860; open summer only, 10am–6pm
• Visitor Centre: Hellnar; 436 6888; open Jun–10 Sep: 10am–6pm daily
• Summer-only buses from Reykjavík to Hellissandur; www.bsi. is, www.west.is
• www.ust.is

Top 10 Features

1. Snæfellsjökull
2. Coastal Boundary
3. Djúpalónssandur
4. Hellnar
5. Dritvík
6. Ascending Snæfellsjökull
7. Bird-Watching
8. Bárður's Statue
9. Hiking the National Park
10. Arnarstapi

Snæfellsjökull
Snæfellsjökull is the 1,445-m- (4,745-ft-) high icecap covering the dormant Snæfell volcano, which last erupted in 250 AD. The white cone of the volcano is clearly visible *(above)* to the north from Reykjavík on a clear day, rising up above Faxaflói Bay.

Coastal Boundary
The rugged coast of the Snæfellsnes Peninsula acts as a barrier between the rougher weather to the north and the generally drier, sunnier south. Strong storms with snowfall on the higher ground are common throughout the year.

Djúpalónssandur
A pretty pebble beach *(main image)* near Dritvík where four heavy stones – Useless, Half Strength, Puny and Full Strength – were once used to test the brawn of applicants for fishing boat crews.

Hellnar
Hometown *(above)* of the first woman to sail to North America, Guðríður Þorbjarnardóttir. She gave birth to the first European born there around AD 1004.

Dritvík
Some 24 km (15 miles) from Hellissandur, this bay *(above)* harboured what was once the area's busiest fishing fleet. It is a good place to take a break and ponder over changing times.

Ascending Snæfellsjökull
Experienced hikers can spend a day climbing Snæfellsjökull on a trail which runs over the mountain via the three-peaked summit. It is also possible to sled up and ski down. Get advice from the Visitor Centre or the National Park office.

Bird-Watching
Unmistakably large white-tailed sea eagles are often seen in the vicinity of Snæfellsjökull National Park, although this rare bird mainly inhabits the West Fjords. Apart from these, the coastline supports the usual sea birds *(above)* and wild fowl.

Bárður's Statue
A terrific split stone statue of folk figure Bárður Snæfellsás stands near Arnarstapi. According to legend, Bárður was an early settler in the area and his protective spirit still lives on Snæfell and watches over the village.

Hiking the National Park
Beginning from Hellissandur, a range of circular hiking trails explore the lava fields and coastline west of Snæfellsjökull. Expect to encounter little beaches, rugged seascapes, rare plants, birdlife and seals.

Journey to the Centre of the Earth

Snæfellsjökull sprang to fame in Jules Verne's novel *Journey to the Centre of the Earth*, in which a German professor and his nephew decode an ancient manuscript and use the instructions to descend into Snæfell's crater on a subterranean journey of exploration. Such craters were traditionally feared here as the literal entrances to hell, a belief which left many mountains unscaled till the 19th century.

Arnarstapi
Set at the foot of Snæfell's southeast, Arnarstapi is another tiny fishing village, where a rocky arch known as Gatklettur stands out to sea. You can also organize snowcat trips onto Snæfellsjökull from here.

top four

⑩ Látrabjarg Bird Cliffs

The Látrabjarg Bird Cliffs are just about as remote a place as you can readily reach in Iceland. Traditionally a farming area, the region has become almost depopulated since the 1960s, leaving Látrabjarg to the millions of seabirds that return here to breed during summer months. Most people come here to see the abundant numbers of charismatic puffins. On the way there is also a worthwhile folk museum and an amazing beach at Breiðavík, probably the last thing you would expect to find in this part of the world.

Hótel Látrabjarg

🚗 The Látrabjarg road is rough gravel, open only in summer. Check your car rental policy before planning a trip. Unless you have experience of similar driving conditions, it is probably best to take a bus from the capital of the West Fjords, Ísafjörður.

🍴 This is a remote area, and the hotel at Breiðavík is the only place near Látrabjarg where you can get a meal.

• Map A2
• Summer-only buses run three times a week from Ísafjörður. Day-returns allow 2 hours and 30 minutes at Látrabjarg; www.bogf.is
• Hnjótur Folk Museum: open 24 May–15 Sep: 10am–6pm daily, by appointment at other times

Top 10 Features

1. Látrabjarg Cliffs
2. Geology
3. Bird Apartments
4. Eggs
5. Puffins
6. Guano
7. Látrabjarg History
8. Bjargtangar
9. Hnjótur Folk Museum
10. Breiðavík

Látrabjarg Cliffs
The 14-km- (9-mile-) long and up to 440-m (1,444-ft) high cliffs form a colossal bird colony with millions of seabirds, puffins, cormorants, kittiwakes, razorbills and guillemots, nesting here every year *(above)*.

Bird Apartments
All the bird species here nest at different heights, forming banded apartments: puffins at the top, then razorbills, fulmars and kittiwakes *(right)*, with guillemots on the narrow sheer cliff ledges.

Geology
Iceland's western extremity is home to its oldest, geological formations. The layered cliffs are a slice through the past, each distinct band – clearly visible despite the birdlife – recording the different volcanic events.

Eggs
Due to their habit of favouring crowded, sheer cliffs, guillemot eggs are conical – a shape which makes them roll in a circle around their tip rather than over the edge.

Látrabjarg has the world's largest razorbill colony.

5 Puffins

The most amiable residents of Látrabjarg are the puffins *(main image)*. These small seabirds have orange feet and a multicoloured, sail-shaped bill. They nest in grassy burrows at the top of the cliffs and often tolerate a cautious approach.

6 Guano

You cannot fail to notice the smell of guano at Látrabjarg. The thick, spongy grass, at the top of the cliffs *(above)* exists thanks to the centuries of fertile guano deposits, without which the puffins would have nowhere to dig their nests.

7 Látrabjarg History

The Látrabjarg cliffs were, until 1926, a favourite summer haunt for local farmers, who scaled the cliffs to collect bird eggs. Puffins were once caught and eaten in large numbers, a practice that continues to this day in the southern islands of Vestmannaeyjar *(see p108)*.

8 Bjargtangar

This westernmost point of Europe is marked by the lonely beacon of the Bjargtangar lighthouse, a small, white-washed and distinctly weatherbeaten building high up on the grassy clifftop. The lighthouse marks the beginning of Látrabjarg cliffs. A warning sign has almost fallen over the edge.

10 Breiðavík

Breiðavík, 15 km (9 miles) from Látrabjarg, features a long, golden beach *(right)* – a rarity here as the sand is usually volcanic black. On a sunny day you could almost imagine yourself in the Mediterranean.

9 Hnjótur Folk Museum

About 50 km (31 miles) from Látrabjarg, this isolated museum provides an insight into the lives of farmers. Do not miss the video of the *Sargon* shipwreck and the aircraft display.

The Wreck of the Sargon

In 1947 a British trawler, *Dhoon* foundered off the Látrabjarg coast in a December storm. Locals scrambled down the frozen cliffs, fired a safety line onto the stricken vessel and winched the seamen to safety. The following year a film crew arrived to make a documentary about the event when another British vessel, *Sargon*, ran aground: the crew were again saved and the whole event was filmed for real.

🔟 Landmannalaugar Area

Landmannalaugar, meaning "Countryman's Bathing Pool," is a lush hot springs area in southern Iceland surrounded by a stark wilderness of snow-streaked mountains, ancient lava fields and flat glacial river valleys. Much of the countryside here has been shaped by Hekla, the country's second most-active volcano. Excellent camping facilities make it a great spot from where to appreciate the rugged interior. It is connected by summer-only buses from Reykjavík. You can also hike here along the exceptional Laugavegur trail.

Horse riding in the Landmannalaugar area

🕐 The hot springs can get very busy at weekends and when the Reykjavík bus arrives between 1 and 3pm. If staying overnight, time your soak carefully to avoid the crowds.

🍴 In July and early August, you can buy burgers, soft drinks and coffee at the Fjallabúð Café, housed in an old bus at the campsite. There are no other places to eat within 50 km (31 miles).

• Map D5
• Mid-Jun–late Aug: Daily buses from Reykjavík and several a week from Skaftafell. Schedule: www.bsi.is
• Open mid-Jun–late Aug
• Book bunkhouses at Landmannalaugar and along Laugavegur hiking trail in advance with the Icelandic Touring Club: www.fi.is • www.landmannalaugar.info

Top 10 Features

1. Hot Springs
2. Mountains
3. Ófærufoss
4. Campsite
5. Laugavegur
6. Ljótipollur
7. Flora
8. Hrafntinnusker
9. Hekla
10. Frostastaðavatn

Hot Springs

Hot springs emerge into a meadow from underneath a 15th-century lava flow, where they mingle with a cooler stream. Wade up this stream *(below)* until the water temperature increases, then sit down for a soak.

Ófærufoss

A beautiful, two-stage waterfall bridged by lava flowing through what looks like a small volcanic crater. Do not get too close to the rim as the soil here is soft.

Mountains

The 945-m- (3,100-ft-) high Bláhnúkur is the main peak overlooking the springs with an hour-long trail to the top. From here you can view the medieval lava field and ever-changing colours of the grey, pink and orange rhyolite hills *(main image)*.

Campsite

The spacious campsite *(left)* has some grassy spots on the side of the stream and more pitches on soft gravel. Showers, toilets and a food preparation area are nearby, along with bins of rocks to weigh down your tent against Landmannalaugar's famous gales.

➲ *Do not forget to bring a swimsuit and a towel.*

Laugavegur

This rewarding, 60-km- (37-mile-) long trail *(left)* from Landmannalaugar to Þórsmörk features volcanic plains, green hills, snow-bound plateaus and freezing rivers. You can camp or use bunkhouses along the way while hiking.

Ljótipollur

Do not let the name, Icelandic for "ugly puddle", put you off visiting this small crater lake, which forms an attractive blue pool sunk inside a bright red scoria depression.

Flora

Look for tiny, hardy flowers contrasting with the dark lava walls near the springs. Pink thrifts, moss campion, purple self-heal, aromatic thyme, white cottongrass *(below)* and violet butterworts are common.

Hrafntinnusker

Hrafntinnusker is a huge "reef" made of obsidian, black volcanic glass, located southwest of Landmannalaugar. Look for weathered outcrops among the lava field and on Bláhnúkur, along with smaller pebbles all over.

Hekla

The Hekla volcano, towering 1,488 m (4,882 ft) over southwest Iceland, has gone off at 10-year intervals in recent times. The road to Landmannalaugar traverses ash dunes and lava fields from the 1970 eruption *(see p113)*.

Frostastaðavatn

Packed with trout, this lake *(below)* around 5 km (3 miles) from Landmannalaugar is a favourite fishing spot. You can hike around the shore in 3 hours, a fairly easy walk except for a stretch over a lava field.

Hiking Laugavegur

The Laugavegur hike isn't especially difficult but you do need to be self-sufficient and prepared against possible bad conditions. Wear warm, weatherproof clothing and hiking boots, carry maps, a compass, and bring your own food as there are no stores along the way. Bunkhouses must be booked in advance. Campsites are laid out at about 15 km (9 mile) intervals and campers need strong tents in good condition along-with cooking gear.

🔟 Jökulsárlón

Jökulsárlón is a broad lagoon on the southeastern coast, where the nose of the Breiðamerkurjökull glacier edges down to the sea. The lagoon formed after the glacier began receeding during the 1940s and today presents a striking scene, filled by a mass of icebergs freshly broken off the glacier. With a deep, black-sand beach behind you and the white mass of Europe's largest icecap, Vatnajökull, on the horizon, Jökulsárlón is a great spot to stretch your legs on the long drive from Vík to Höfn.

Close-up of glacier ice

🪟 All buses travelling along the south coast stop at Jökulsárlón for around 30 minutes, which is long enough to take in the lagoon and walk down to the sea to look at the ice boulders.

🍽 The café at the Visitor Centre opens 9am–7pm through summer, serving inexpensive waffles, soup of the day and coffee.

• Map G5
• Visitor Centre: open 15 May–15 Sep
• www.randburg.com/is/jokulsarlon

Top 10 Features

1. The Lagoon
2. The Beach
3. Icebergs
4. Vatnajökull
5. Aquatic Life
6. Breiðárlón
7. In the Movies
8. Birds
9. Visitor Centre
10. Boat Tour

The Lagoon

Around 5 km (3 miles) across and fairly narrow, it is the deepest lagoon in Iceland *(main image)*. By contrast, its outflow, the Jökulsá, is the country's shortest river.

Icebergs

The pale blue icebergs create a natural sculpture exhibition *(above)*, constantly changing shape as they melt, breaking into smaller floes. Eventually they are small enough to float to the sea.

The Beach

Over the highway, it is just a short walk to where translucent, weirdly-shaped boulders of ice – the smaller, depleted remains of Jökulsárlón's icebergs – wash downstream to the sea. There they get stranded on the black-sand beach making for some evocative photographs.

Vatnajökull

The lagoon is a good spot to get a feel for Vatnajökull's vast size *(left)*; Breiðamerkurjökull is 15 km (9 miles) across but even this is only a fraction of the massive white icefield before you *(see pp18–19)*.

5 Aquatic Life
Jökulsárlón's cool, deep waters attract herring and trout, which in turn make it a good place to see seals – often spotted snoozing on ice floes *(above)*. Mighty orca or killer whales also visit on occasion.

6 Breiðárlón
For similar scenery but a far more remote atmosphere, head to Breiðárlón, which is 6 km (4 miles) west of Jökulsárlón along the highway and then 3 km (2 miles) north on a gravel road.

7 In the Movies
Movie buffs may well have seen the area even before they visit since Jökulsárlón has featured in two Bond films, a Tomb Raider and a Batman film. It is also a popular place to shoot Icelandic TV commercials.

8 Birds
Bird lovers should look out for the ground-nesting Arctic terns *(above)* and the bulkier brown Arctic skuas. Both have a habit of dive-bombing anything that gets too close to their nests.

9 Visitor Centre
Jökulsárlón's small Visitor Centre *(right)* has a café selling fast food and hot drinks, and a few shelves of souvenir postcards and T-shirts. Climb the black hillock out front for great views of the lagoon.

Bridging the Rivers

Bridging the numerous deep, ever-shifting glacial rivers which thread their way seawards all along the south coast was such a massive undertaking that the national highway around the country – the Ringroad – got completed only in 1974. Before this, places like Jökulsárlón were well off the beaten track, as the main road between Skaftafell and Reykjavík was, in reality, just a gravel track.

10 Boat Tour
For a chance to enter the maze of icebergs right up against the glacier snout, take the 30-minute amphibious boat tours *(below)* at the Visitor Centre. With luck you might also get close to the seals.

Left **Þingvellir, site of Iceland's first Parliament** Right **Ólafur Tryggvason**

⁙10 Moments in History

1 AD 860: Viking Exploration

Around this time a Viking named Naddoður discovered an uninhabited coastline north-east of the Faroe Islands. This new land was later visited by Norseman Flóki Vilgerðarson, who, having spent a harsh winter here, named it "Ísland" (Iceland).

Viking explorer Naddoður discovers Iceland

2 AD 870: Reykjavík Settled

Norwegians Ingólfur Arnarson and Hjörleifur Hróðmarsson set sail for Iceland with their families. Hjörleifur was murdered by his slaves after he settled at Hjörleifshöfði. Ingólfur became Iceland's first permanent settler, building his homestead at a place he named Reykjavík (Smoky Bay).

3 AD 930: Alþing Established at Þingvellir

All available land in Iceland was settled by AD 930 and regional chieftains found it necessary to form a national government. Rejecting the idea of a king, they opted for a Commonwealth. The Parliament (Alþing) was convened annually at Þingvellir, where laws were made and disputes settled.

4 AD 1000: Iceland Becomes Catholic

The majority of Iceland's original settlers believed in Norse gods. During the 10th century, however, Norway's king Ólafur Tryggvason threatened Iceland with invasion unless it converted to Christianity. Accordingly, the Alþing of AD 1000 adopted Catholicism as Iceland's official religion.

5 1262: The Old Treaty with Norway

During the 13th century, power moved into the hands of wealthy landowners, who plunged the island into civil war. Norway stepped in as peacemaker, and in 1262 Iceland accepted Norwegian sovereignty as a semi-independent state under the Old Treaty.

6 1397: Denmark Takes Over

Denmark's ruler, the "Lady King" Margrete, absorbed the Norwegian throne under the Kalmar Union. Later on, Denmark rejected Iceland's claims of autonomy, and in 1661, used military force to impose absolute rule.

7 1550: Iceland Becomes Lutheran

The Danish king appointed Gissur Einarsson as Iceland's first Lutheran bishop in 1542. As the nation reluctantly adopted the new faith, Iceland's last Catholic bishop, Jón Arason, took up arms. He was defeated at Skálholt and executed on 7 November, 1550.

8 1783: Lakagígar Eruption

A major volcanic eruption along the Laki craters flooded southeastern Iceland with lava. Poisonous fallout then wiped out agriculture across the land. Famine over the next three years killed one in three Icelanders, and Denmark considered evacuating the entire country to Jutland.

9 1874: The Nationalist Movement

The mid-19th century saw a swelling of nationalism in Iceland and a challenge to Denmark's authority. The movement was led by poet Jónas Hallgrímsson and historian Jón Sigurðsson. This culminated in the Danish king Christian IX ratifying a new constitution in 1874, which returned legislative power to the Alþing.

10 1944: Iceland Declares Independence

Denmark's invasion by Nazi Germany in 1940 nullified its territorial rule over Iceland, and the Alþing decided to declare independence. Political squabbles confused the process but on 17 June 1944 the country's first president, Sveinn Björnsson, proclaimed Icelandic Independence at Þingvellir, marking the end of 700 years of foreign rule.

Line of Lakagígar craters

Top 10 Figures in Icelandic History

1 Flóki Vilgerðarson
The Viking who named Iceland and was known as Hrafna-Flóki, or Raven-Flóki, after his pet birds.

2 Ingólfur Arnarson
Iceland's first official settler, who left his native Norway following a feud with the local earl.

3 Leifur Eiríksson
Son of Eirík the Red, Leifur sailed west from Greenland in 1000 and discovered America.

4 Guðríður Þorbjarnardóttir
Mother of the first European born in North America, she later made a pilgrimage to Rome.

5 Snorri Sturlurson
The 13th-century historian, politician and author of *Egil's Saga*, the *Heimskringla* and the *Prose Edda*.

6 Jón Sigurðsson
Leader of the independence movement, he promoted the move for Iceland's political autonomy from Denmark.

7 Jónas Hallgrímsson
Influential Romantic poet who shaped nationalist pride during the 1800s.

8 Hannes Hafsteinn
Iceland's first Home Minister in 1904, who oversaw a period of modernization and social change.

9 Vigdís Finnbogadóttir
Iceland's president from 1980 until 1996, and the first democratically elected female head of state.

10 Jóhanna Sigurðardóttir
The world's first gay political leader, who became the prime minister of Iceland in January 2009.

Left **Gullfoss** Right **Camp at the foot of Dynjandi falls**

🔟 Waterfalls

1 Dettifoss
Europe's biggest waterfall in terms of volume, this monster at Jökulsárgljúfur National Park in northeastern Iceland can be heard miles away. The stark setting, where the river drops 45 m (148 ft) between the shattered cliffs of the Jökulsá canyon, adds to the spectacle. Upstream is another fall, Selfoss, only 10 m (33 ft) high but 70 m (230 ft) across. ◈ *Map F2*

2 Glymur
Iceland's tallest waterfall, Glymur drops nearly 200 m (658 ft) off the top of a plateau inland from Hvalfjörður, along the west coast. Legend has it that a mythical beast, half man and half whale, swam up the waterfall and into Hvalvatn, the lake at the top – where whale bones have indeed been found. ◈ *Map C4*

3 Gullfoss
This large, beautiful and always impressive two-tier fall sits on the River Hvítá around 75 km (47 miles) northeast from Reykjavík. It is one of Iceland's most visited sights, along with nearby Geysir and Þingvellir. In the early 20th century it was at the heart of the country's first environmental dispute *(see pp14–15)*.

4 Seljalandsfoss
Fed by the melting water from Eyjafjallajökull icecap, Seljalandsfoss is narrow and not especially tall but drops into a meadow along the south coast with surprising force. The path behind the water curtain is muddy and slippery, and a walk along this provides for a good soak. Look out for several smaller falls nearby. ◈ *Map D6*

5 Hraunfossar & Barnafoss
Two adjacent falls within easy reach of Borgarnes on the west coast, with very different characters. At Hraunfossar, blue water splashes out from under a

Streams splashing down a moss-covered bank, Hraunfossar

moss-covered lava bank and gurgles down into the river, while Barnafoss forms a short, savage set of rapids as it cuts through a narrow canyon just upstream. ✎ *Map C4*

Skógafoss
Just walking up along the river to this mighty waterfall is an incredible experience: as you approach, the flat gravel plain vanishes inside soaking clouds of spray and a deafening level of noise. Climb a staircase up to the top for more cascades and views out over southern Iceland's coastline. ✎ *Map D6*

Skógafoss

Dynjandi
This pretty tumble in the West Fjords near Hrafnseyri cascades over several tiers of granite boulders in a 60-m- (198-ft-) wide, 100-m (329-ft) drop. Crashing over all those boulders gives Dynjandi (the Thunderer) its name, but views seawards over grassy dales make it a beautiful place to camp out. ✎ *Map B2*

Goðafoss
Located between Akureyri and Mývatn, this "Waterfall of the Gods" is where the 10th-century lawspeaker Þorgeir Ljósvetningagoði, who champion-ed the introduction of Christianity to Iceland, disposed of the statues of pagan Norse gods in 1000. The ice-blue water channels over several falls, with easy walking tracks between them. ✎ *Map E2*

Aldeyjarfoss
Off the northern end of the rugged Sprengisandur Route across Iceland's interior, Aldeyjarfoss cuts a rough scar across the huge Suðurárhraun lava field, exposing layers of ash and rock settled over successive eruptions. Although only 20 m (66 ft) high, the falls are very forceful and perk up an other-wise lifeless terrain. ✎ *Map E3*

Ófærufoss
This waterfall is associated with the Eldgjá canyon on Fjallabak Route between Landmannalaugar and Skaftafell. The river flows along the top and drops into the canyon, gouging out a broad, scree-ridden pool before falling again as a smaller curtain on to the plain. ✎ *Map E5*

Left **Arctic skua** Centre **Whale-watching vessel** Right **Látrabjarg cliffs**

🔟 Places to See Birds and Wildlife

1 Lake Mývatn

The country's top venue for viewing wildlife, Lake Mývatn slots easily into a trip to see Iceland's laid-back northern capital, Akureyri, and a whale-watching expedition from Húsavík. Ducks and other wildfowl are the main draws, but the elusive Arctic fox and gyrfalcon are also regularly encountered *(see pp16–17)*.

2 Látrabjarg

Way out in the West Fjords, a trip to Látrabjarg takes a little bit of planning but you will not forget your first sight of these cliffs, covered by enormous, noisy colonies of nesting sea-birds. Stop along the way for a walk or sunbathe on Breiðavík Beach *(see pp22–3)*.

3 Hornbjarg

At 533 m (1,749 ft), Hornbjarg is the highest clifftop on the isolated, completely unin-habited Hornstrandir Peninsula, on the West Fjords' extreme northwest. Like Látrabjarg, it is teeming with millions of fulmars, kittiwakes, razorbills and guille-mots, but to get here you will have to catch irregular boats from Ísafjörður and then hike back over several days. ◎ *Map B1*

4 Dyrhólaey

The grassy, sculptured headland of Dyrhólaey is an easy detour off the highway between Skógar and Vík. Apart from close encounters with puffins and other seabirds, come here to view the black, volcanic-sand beaches and the huge sea arch, large enough for a ship to sail through. ◎ *Map D6*
• *Closed 1 May–25 Jun*

Razorbill at the Látrabjarg cliffs

5 Jökulsárlón

One of the most spellbinding sights of southeastern Iceland, this deep, iceberg-filled lagoon between the sea and Breiðamerkurjökull glacier is a great place to spot seals and orca, if you are lucky. The sandy plains on either side are full of nesting terns and skuas – and Arctic foxes looking for a meal *(see pp26–7)*.

6 Skjálfandi

A summer sailing trip out from Húsavík to Skjálfandi, the broad bay offshore, is certain to put you within viewing range of marine mammals. You are most likely to see seals and dolphins but with luck you will encounter the spectacular humpback whales leaping out of the water. ◎ *Map E2*

The elusive Arctic fox

Tiny islands in Breiðafjörður

Breiðafjörður
7 The waters off the west coast are dotted with hundreds of islets and skerries inhabited by thousands of puffins, shags, cormorants and other seabirds. White-tailed sea eagles, one of Iceland's rare and majestic birds, are also seen here. ◈ *Map B3*

Garðskagi
8 Close to Keflavík International Airport, this little tongue of land overlooks a gravelly beach where you can easily spot redshank, sanderlings, turnstones, eider duck and other shorebirds – look out to sea for gannets. The striped rod lighthouse was once used to monitor bird migration. ◈ *Map B5*

Ingólfshöfði
9 This narrow, sandy spit of land between Vík and Höfn is said to be where Iceland's first settler, Ingólfur Arnarson, landed. Fearless puffins and greater skua nest here in summer, when tractor tours trundle out from the highway. ◈ *Map F5 • Hofsnes Farm • 894 0894 • Tractor tours: Apr–Oct Mon–Sat at noon; groups by appointment • Adm*

Þjórsárver
10 This extensive expanse of protected, mossy wetland along Iceland's largest river, the 230-km- (143-mile-) long Þjórsá, is where most of the world's pink-footed geese raise their young. Whooper swan, snipe and greylag geese live alongside. ◈ *Map E4*

Top 10 Icelandic Birds

1 Puffin
This charismatic bird nests in burrows on grassy sea cliffs around Iceland between May and September.

2 Arctic Tern
A small, graceful seabird which fearlessly dive-bombs anything which gets too close to its nest.

3 Gyrfalcon
A rare, grey-white falcon which once featured on Iceland's coat of arms. Seek them out around Mývatn.

4 Golden Plover
Common grassland bird whose piping call is eagerly awaited by Icelanders as heralding the spring.

5 Raven
Huge black crow with a harsh call and acrobatic flight, considered highly intelligent by many Icelanders.

6 Meadow Pipit
The island's most abundant bird is a sweet songster, though it can be surprisingly hard to see.

7 White-tailed Sea Eagle
Once persecuted by farmers as a pest, around 80 white-tailed sea eagles now breed in the northwest.

8 Eider Duck
Pied sea duck known for its soft, warm down. It is common around the coast and on lakes inland.

9 Ptarmigan
Grouse renowned for its unique, snow-white winter plumage. A popular Christmas dish in Iceland.

10 Harlequin Duck
Sea duck with an unmistakable blue and red plumage. It breeds inland from May to July around fast-flowing streams.

Left **Greens at a Reykjavík golf club** Right **Borgarnes**

Places to Play Golf

1 Hólmsvöllur
An 18-hole, par-72 course on Iceland's westernmost peninsula, Hólmsvöllur is famous for its sunset views and birdlife. It is a challenging course overall, but the 3rd hole is Iceland's most notorious, requiring a 200-m (660-ft) drive over the sea.
❧ Map B5 • Suðurnes, 232 Keflavík • 421 4100 • Adm • www.golf.is/gs

2 Garðabær
There are three golf courses in Reykjavík's Garðabær suburb, including the 18-hole, par-71 Urriðavöllur and Ljúflingur's easier 9-hole, par-3 course. They are open quite late (until 10pm) through June and July, taking advantage of the long daylight hours. ❧ Map P6 • Urriðavöllur, Garðabær • 565 9092 • Adm • www. oddur.is, www.midnightgolf.is

Putting at a course in Garðabær

3 Korpúlfsstaðir
Tailored into what was once the sprawling Korpúlfsstaðir farmstead, "Korpá" is an 18-hole, par-72 course set in splendid scenery. Half of the well-wooded course is played along the seafront with Reykjavík's Esja plateau rising beyond, while the rest follows the banks of the Korpá river. The 12th and 15th holes are the toughest. ❧ Map Q5 • Korpúlfsstaðir, 112 Reykjavík • 585 0200 • Adm • www.grgolf.is/english

4 Keilir
This club, located 30 km (19 miles) from Reykjavík among Hafnarfjörður's extensive lava fields, is named after the distinct conical mountain rising behind it. Hvaleyrarvöllur, the main 18-hole green is rated par-71, with strong winds from the Atlantic as perhaps the biggest hazard – you need accuracy here, not just power. There is also a 9-hole practice course. ❧ Map B5 • Steinholti 1, 220 Hafnarfjörður • 565 3360 • Adm • www.keilir.is (Icelandic only)

5 Borgarnes
If the golfing options near Reykjavík are too crowded, drive an hour along the west coast to Borgarnes town and its 18-hole, par-71 green, Hamarsvöllur. It is nicely landscaped, with plenty of natural water hazards and the distant hills framing the course add to its charm. ❧ Map B4 • Hamarsvöllur, 310 Borgarnes • 437 1663 • Adm • www.golf.is/gb

All golf courses in Iceland are open to the public.

Golfers at the Akureyri greens

Akureyri

The world's most northerly 18-hole course, Akureyri's par-71 green is set in wild, open moorland, though stands of trees and rocky outcrops are used to break up the terrain. The annual Arctic Open is held here in June, with tee-offs after midnight against the glowing midsummer night skies.
🆂 Map E2 • Jaðar, 600 Akureyri • 462 2074, 096 0814 • Adm • www.gagolf.is (Icelandic only), www.arcticopen.is

Fljótsdalshérað

A popular 9-hole, par-68 course in the suburb of Fellabær, Fljótsdalshérað hosts the East Iceland Open in July. Ormurinn, a giant, snake-like monster, is said to inhabit adjacent Lögurinn lake.
🆂 Map G3 • Fljótsdalshérað, Fellabær, 700 Egilsstaðir • 471 1113 (summer only) • Adm • golfvollur@simnet.is

Vestmannaeyjar

Founded in 1938, this 18-hole, par-70 course is one of the most dramatic. To the north are the steep, grassy slopes of a collapsed volcano cone; westwards, the green drops into the sea; while to the east is the Eldfell volcano, still steaming after its 1973 eruption. The

Volcano Open is held here in July.
🆂 Map C6 • Heimaey, Vestmannaeyjar • 481 2363 • Adm • www.gvgolf.is

Krossdalsvöllur

As if there wasn't enough to do around Mývatn – birdwatching, volcano climbing, visiting hot pools and boiling mud pits – there is this 9-hole, par-33 course too. Apart from the hazards, try not to confuse bird eggs for lost golf balls. 🆂 Map F2 • Stekkholti, 660 Mývatn • 856 1159 • Adm • stekkholt@emax.is

Geysir Golf Course

Opened in 2006, just a long tee shot from the famous hot springs, this L-shaped, 9-hole, par-37 course is gaining a reputation as one of the best-designed in the country, landscaped carefully using the natural vegetation. The club also sports a driving range.
🆂 Map C5 • Haukadalur, 801 Selfoss • 486 8733 • Adm • www.geysirgolf.is

Left **Hverfjall's gravel cone** Right **Crater lake, Lakagígar**

Volcanoes

1 Hekla

This large, lively mountain has erupted over a dozen times since Settlement, most famously burying a host of nearby Viking farms under ash in 1104. The last major stirrings were in the 1940s, but there have been many smaller incidents since then. In between eruptions, experienced hikers can walk to the top *(see p113)*.

2 Katla

This dangerous volcano lies buried beneath the Mýrdalsjökull icecap near Skógar on the south coast. It erupts on average at a 70-year interval, and the last one, in 1918, sent a titanic flood of meltwater and gravel down nearby valleys. Recent activity in the area might be signalling an awakening. ◈ *Map D6*

3 Snæfell

This stratovolcano – one whose cone has built up gradually over successive eruptions – is believed to have last erupted around AD 250 and today is covered by the Snæfellsjökull icecap *(see pp20–21)*. Unlike Hekla, whose top is usually shrouded by cloud, Snæfell's bright white peak stands like a beacon over the west coast. ◈ *Map A4*

4 Öræfajökull

Iceland's tallest volcano is located near Ingólfshöfði. Its terrible explosion in 1362 buried almost a third of the country under gravel and forced the abandonment of farms all along the south coast. Another eruption in 1727 caused less damage mainly because only a few people had returned to live here. ◈ *Map F5*

5 Lakagígar

In 1783, the countryside inland from Kirkjubæjarklaustur split open a huge rent, which belched fire and poisonous fumes for seven months. It is said that Kirkjubæjarklaustur itself was saved by the actions

View of the Snæfellsjökull icecap, Snæfell

of pastor Jón Steingrímsson, who bundled the town's population into the church and prayed that they be spared – the lava halted right at the church boundary *(see p114)*.

6 Eldfell

The 1973 eruption of Eldfell on Heimaey, in the Westman Islands, buried a third of the town under lava and the rest under 3 m (10 ft) of ash. But the harbour was saved – and even improved – by the spraying seawater on to the lava front as it edged down from the volcano. ◈ *Map C6*

7 Krafla

The Krafla Fires of 1975-84, northeast of Mývatn, happened at a bad time: Leirbotn Geothermal Power Station was under construction and the fires delayed its completion for over a decade. However, the new source of natural heat might make it possible to increase the station's projected 60 MW output *(see p17)*.

8 Grímsvötn

Currently Iceland's most active volcano, Grímsvötn smoulders away 400 m (1,315 ft) below the massive Vatnajökull icecap. The system was responsible for the Lakagígar event of 1783 and, more recently, a massive *jökulhlaup* – a volcanically-induced flash flood – that tore out from under the Skeiðarárjökull in 1995, destroying several bridges. ◈ *Map E4*

9 Hverfjall

A tall and broad gravel cone east of Lake Mývatn that was

Hot pool at Krafla's base

created around 500 BC during geological upheavals, Hverfjall is now extinct. Lava on the lower slopes is from the remains of the flows of a separate volcano which erupted around 1000. The summit is a relatively easy climb and provides wide views of the lake *(see pp16–17)*.

10 Askja

During the winter of 1875, an apparently small vent in the massive Askja caldera exploded with such force that it vapourized two cubic kilometres of rock, which fell as a thick layer of pumice all across northeastern Iceland. With their farms buried, many of the local residents emigrated to Canada. Askja last erupted in 1961. ◈ *Map F3*

Left **Vox** Centre **Signage of Gullfoss** Right **La Primavera**

 Places for Fine Dining

1 Grillið

This old, elegant, beautifully furnished rooftop restaurant on the eighth floor of the Radisson Hotel offers some of the best food in Reykjavík. Top marks go to their turbot with Jerusalem artichokes and salt cod with lobster tails. Enjoy an aperitif – and the cityscape – from their Astra Bar. ✆ Map J3 • Radisson SAS Saga, Hagatorg, 107 Reykjavík • 525 9960
• Open 6:30pm–11:30pm Tue–Sat • kkkkk

2 Perlan

You can't help but be impressed with Perlan's setting: a revolving restaurant under a glass dome with fantastic vistas over the city. Service is excellent and the food good, if not always as outstanding as the location – the grilled lamb fillet is reliable, as are venison dishes. ✆ Map M6
• Öskjuhlíð, 105 Reykjavík • 562 0200
• Open 6:30pm–10:30pm • kkkk

3 Gallery

The island's most swanky diner, with a lobby full of fine Icelandic artworks and French-trained chef Friðgeir Eiríksson at the helm. Service is faultless and the menu based on classic French cuisine: go for the fried monkfish and fennel. Extensive but pricey wine list. ✆ Map L3
• Hótel Holt, Bergstaðastræti 37, 101 Reykjavík • 552 5700
• Open 7:30–11am, noon–2pm, 6:30–10:30pm • kkkkk

4 Vox

Stylish and innovative, this restaurant heads the trend in sourcing fresh Icelandic ingredients – seafood straight off the trawlers, game meats from specialist farms and charr fished locally. Their bistro offers a relatively inexpensive daily lunch buffet. ✆ Map R4
• Hilton Reykjavík Nordica, Suðurlandsbraut 2, 108 Reykjavík • 444 5050 • Open 6:30–10:30pm Wed–Sat • kkkk

5 Argentína Steikhús

Visit this carnivorous den for charr-grilled entrecôte, ribeye, T-bone or tenderloin steaks sourced from Icelandic cattle, washed down with heavy red wine. They also serve chicken, lamb and seafood. Try a dessert and cognac. ✆ Map M4 • Barónsstígur 11a • 551 9555
• Open 6pm–midnight Sun–Thu, 5:30pm–1am Fri–Sat • kkkkk

6 Domo

An arty restaurant with a black, red and white decor and an

The elegant interior of Gallery

A bottle of fine wine costs the same as a meal for one.

above average Asian fusion menu. Pan-fried scallops are perfect and it is probably the only place outside Melbourne that cooks kangaroo without drying it *(see p77)*.

7 La Primavera
Classic Italian restaurant famed for its excellent, tasty and filling favourites such as beef carpaccio, gnocchi with ceps mushrooms, flounder with tomato pesto and chicken risotto. Their desserts are wonderful – the warmed chocolate cake with ice cream is legendary. ⊗ *Map L2*
• *Austurstræti 9, 101 Reykjavík • 561 8555*
• *Open 11:30am–2pm, 6–10:30pm Tue-Fri, 6–11:30pm Sat • kkkk*

8 Fiskmarkaðurinn
"The Fish Market" is Asian and the sushi outstanding. Like several top-notch restaurants, they source local produce where possible. The smart décor matches the meal. ⊗ *Map K2*
• *Aðalstræti 12, 101 Reykjavík • 578 8877*
• *Open 11:30am–2pm, 6–11:30pm • kkkkk*

9 Sjávarkjallarinn
Believed to serve the best seafood in all Iceland, this very expensive and chic restaurant specializes in Asian-European fusion dishes: the monkfish with truffle and artichoke is outstanding. ⊗ *Map K2 • Aðalstræti 2, 101 Reykjavík • 511 1212 • Open 6–10:30pm Sun–Thu, 6–11:30pm Fri–Sat • kkkkk*

10 Fjöruborðið
Famed for its lobster, this restaurant is located in an old timber building in Stokkseyri, an hour's drive from Reykjavík. The rest of the menu features lamb and other local stalwarts. Book in advance. ⊗ *Map C5 • Eyrarbraut 3a, Stokkseyri • 899 9494 • Open summer: noon–10pm daily, winter: 6–9pm Wed–Thu noon–10pm Sat–Sun • kkkk*

Top 10 Icelandic Foods

1 Lamb
The mainstay of Icelandic cuisine, lamb is eaten fresh, smoked, turned into sausages, or preserved in whey after pressing.

2 Lobster
Superb and plentiful, best served as tails with butter and, perhaps, a little garlic seasoning or cream.

3 Salmon
Wild-caught Atlantic salmon is firm and rich; usually served smoked or marinated with herbs as butter-soft *graflax*.

4 Caviar
Iceland's supplies come from capelin and lumpfish, not the classic sturgeon, but are just as delicious.

5 Cod
Most often snacked on as dried, chewy *harðfiskur*, but also cooked fresh and used in soups.

6 Hákarl
Greenland shark, fermented in sand for six months to break down toxins. Eye-wateringly strong.

7 Brennivín
Icelandic vodka, flavoured with caraway seeds and affectionately known locally as "Black Death". Use sparingly.

8 Skyr
Like a thick, set yoghurt, available in any supermarket in a range of flavours.

9 Arctic Charr
Freshwater fish with a beautifully subtle flavour. The best come from Þingvallavatn and Mývatn.

10 Ptarmigan
Plump partridge-like bird which takes the place of turkey in Iceland at traditional Christmas meals.

Left **Fish & Chips** Right **Interior of Jómfrúin**

Cheaper Eats in Reykjavík

Á Næstu Grösum
You don't have to be a vegetarian to enjoy a meal at this old, friendly vegetarian restaurant with cheerful decor. Ingredients are sourced from organic farms, and the cafeteria-style menu always has vegan and Indian options. Large servings and relatively low prices are another plus. ◈ *Map L3* • *Laugavegur 20b* • *552 8410* • *Open 11:30am–10pm Mon–Sat, 5–10pm Sun* • *kk*

Basil & Lime restaurant

Garðurinn
Small vegetarian café with a set menu that changes weekly. They offer a range of crêpes, flans, stews and pastas, but their forte is tasty soups (served with bread) and quiches. The "dish of the day" plus soup is excellent value. Great coffee and cakes too. ◈ *Map M2* • *Klapparstígur 37* • *561 2345* • *Open 11am–6:30pm Mon–Tue & Thu–Fri, 11am–5pm Wed, noon–5pm Sat* • *k*

Jómfrúin
Calling this place a Danish sandwich shop does not do it justice: a good smørrebrød (open sandwich) involves a choice of prawns, herring, smoked lamb, cheese and countless other garnishes served on a thick slice of heavy rye bread, and Jómfrúin delivers in style. Do include the fried plaice in your selection. ◈ *Map L2* • *Lækjargata 4* • *551 0100* • *Open 11am–6pm daily* • *kk*

Basil & Lime
The bright yellow exterior hides a subdued restaurant which offers hearty, well-presented Italian fare – antipasto, lobster tagliatelle and home-made *tiramisu* (the house specialities) will leave your palate and stomach content. The patio is nice on warm days. ◈ *Map M3* • *Klapparstígur 38* • *555 3696* • *Open 11:30am–10pm Mon–Thu, 11:30am–11pm Fri–Sat, 5–10pm Sun* • *kkk*

Turninn (Nineteen)
Nineteen opens only for lunch and is getting a name for its generous buffets for the weekend brunch – soup, salads, eggs, bacon, steak and chocolate cake. This restaurant is located on the 19th floor of "The Tower", Iceland's tallest building, a glass highrise in Reykjavík's Kópavogur suburb. ◈ *Map Q5* • *Smáratorg 3, 201 Kópavogur* • *575 7500* • *Open 11:30am–2pm Mon–Fri, 11am–2pm Sat–Sun* • *kkk*

Jómfrúin

For more restaurants **See pp40–41, 77.**

6 Búllan

Standing isolated on a corner at the harbour entrance inside a 1950s concrete shell, this tiny, glass-fronted diner does just one thing – burgers – and does them extremely well. A great place if you need a cheap, decent, filling meal after staggering off a whale-watching boat. Always busy, so be prepared to queue up. ◈ Map K1 • Geirsgata 1 • 511 1888 • Open 11:30am–9pm daily • k

7 Krúa Thai

One of the few places left in Iceland where you can get an economical, real restaurant meal – even if it's only a single course. All your old favourites, from panang curry to tom kha gai, served in a relaxed, fast-food ambience. The beer is not too expensive either. ◈ Map L2 • Tryggvagata 14 • 561 0039 • Open 11:30am–9:30pm Mon–Fri, 2–9:30pm Sat, 5–9:30pm Sun • k

8 Fish & Chips

Up at Reykjavík's old harbour, this tidy café delivers just what it says: choose from Icelandic cod, plaice, halibut or "catfish" served with a variety of flavoured mayonnaise and oven-grilled chips. Everything is organic, tasty and well cooked. ◈ Map K2 • Tryggvagata 8 • 511 1118 • Open 11:30am–9pm Mon–Fri, noon–9pm Sat & Sun • kk

9 Þrír Frakkar

Set in a warm, pink building in a quiet residential area, the "Three Overcoats" specializes in seafood, with excellent trout, lobster, and soups served in a French-Asian fusion. The

Þrír Frakkar

whale steak, pan-fried guillemot breast, smoked puffin and horse tenderloin are cooked in traditional Icelandic style. ◈ Map L3 • Baldursgata 14 • 552 3939 • Open 11:30am–2:30pm & 6–10pm Mon–Fri, 6–11pm Sat & Sun • kkkk

10 Ítalía

Unpretentious Italian restaurant that has been around for years and manages to deliver satisfying, enjoyably tasty portions of pasta, pollo and pizza in a good-natured, homey environment. Hard to single any one dish out, but their parma ham pizza, penne à la arrabiatta and baccala are a cut above other dishes. ◈ Map L2 • Laugavegur 11 • 552 4630 • Open 11:30am–11:30pm daily • kkk

Left **Signage of Café Oliver, Reykjavík** Right **Kaffi Amor, Akureyri**

Bars, Clubs and Cafés

NASA

Any serious night out in Reykjavík has to involve NASA at some point; a few come for the bar but it is the weekend bands – or a DJ at the very least – which really pack the place out. This is Iceland's best nightclub for loud, live music, showcasing local and foreign talent. Bring warm clothing for you may have to queue in the snow for your turn to get in. *Map L2 • Við Austurvöllur, 101 Reykjavík • 511 1313 • Cover charge for bands • www.nasa.is*

B5

Laid-back café by day (with a proper library), B5 is another multi-function venue which transforms into a popular bar-club after dark. Complete with two private lounges (one built in an old bank vault), if you are planning a party. *Map L2 • Bankastræti 5, 101 Reykjavík • 552 9600 • Open 10:30am–midnight Mon–Wed, 10:30–1am Thu, 10:30–4:30am Fri–Sun*

Café Oliver

This is more a restaurant than a café, with an Indian-influenced menu offered from lunchtime (when daily specials are good value) until 10pm. Once the kitchen closes, the bar and music fires up: live bands perform Tuesday and Thursday nights, with DJs on weekends. *Map M2 • Laugavegur 20a, 101 Reykjavík • 552 2300 • Open 11:45–1am Mon–Thu, 11:45–4:30am Fri, 3pm–4:30am Sat, 3pm–1am Sun*

Thorvaldsen Bar

Difficult to know whether Thorvaldsen's is really a restaurant, a bar or a club, as it does each fairly well. The food is Asian fusion and is served in a Nordic setting. The bar is well-stocked and the music is aimed at the crowd which floods in after 11pm. *Map L2 • Austurstræti 8, 101 Reykjavík • 511 1413 • Open 11am–1pm Mon–Thu, 11am–5pm Fri, 11am–6pm Sat*

Hverfisbarinn

It is hard to believe that Hverfisbarinn's bland exterior whitewash and a 1950s-style signage – hides a stylish, moody bar and nightclub, with a mix of live music and DJs pulling in a young, enthusiastic crowd after 10pm on Thursday, Friday and Saturday. It stays open very late on the weekends throughout the

The bar at B5, Reykjavík

Nightclubs do not get going until 11pm.

summer. 🌑 Map L2 • Hverfisgata 20, 101 Reykjavík • 699 1105 • Open 8pm–5:30am Thu–Sat

6 Kaffi Sólon

Smart corner café on the city's main shopping street, Kaffi Sólon has window seating and, on sunny days, streetside seating for people-watching. It is packed at lunchtime but quietens down through the afternoon, though the bar picks up again after dark. It transforms into a popular nightclub on the weekends, with DJ-driven dance tunes. 🌑 Map L2 • Bankastræti 7a, 101 Reykjavík • 565 3232 • Open 11am–midnight Mon–Wed, 11–1am Thu–Sat, noon–midnight Sun

7 Sjallinn

The DJs do their best in the tiny top-floor nightclub as half of Akureyri packs in to Sjallinn at weekends. The major bands get to play on the sound stage downstairs, just about the biggest music venue in town. Either way, a top place for a night on the town. 🌑 Map E2 • Geislagata 14, Akureyri • 462 2770 • Open midnight–4am Fri–Sat, 10pm–1am Thu

8 Kaffi Amor

Set right on the "circle", Akureyri's downtown square, Kaffi Amor is about the only café outside Reykjavík which can really claim a touch of the city's chic ambiance. A great place just to hang out over a coffee during the day, making use of the outdoor seating and just watching the crowds. After dark, come for a beer, occasional bands or just to watch major sports events on TV. 🌑 Map E2 • Ráðhústorg, Akureyri • 461 3030 • Open 2pm–1am Mon–Thu

Dubliner, Reykjavík

9 Dubliner

In terms of atmosphere and decibels, the lively Dubliner is simply a clone of all the other Irish pubs. Nonetheless, after a few pints of Guiness it hardly matters, and it is a reliable place to warm up before heading to NASA. 🌑 Map L2 • Hafnarstræti 4, 101 Reykjavík • 511 3232 • Open 5pm–1am Mon–Thu, 3pm–5:30am Fri–Sat

10 Kaffibarinn

The distinctive corrugated red iron exterior, just off Reykjavík's main shopping area, conceals Kaffibarinn's dark interior with cable-top candles and arty magazines. It is a trendy and popular place to meet up for the first beer of the evening. It hosts pub bands from time to time. 🌑 Map L3 • Bergstaðastræti 1, 101 Reykjavík • 551 1588 • Open 3pm–1am Sun–Thu, 3pm–5am Fri–Sat

Left **Feeding ducks, Tjörnin** Centre **Young girl riding a horse** Right **Bæjarins Bestu wagon**

🔟 Things to Do With Kids

1 Go Swimming

Swimming pools are great places for children to burn off excess energy, especially after long car journeys. Just about every town in Iceland has a heated pool, making it an easy option. Though most of the pools are outdoors, they are especially fun in winter, when snow is falling.

2 Feed the Birds at Tjörnin

In Reykjavík, pick up a loaf of bread from the nearest bakery and head to Tjörnin *(see p74)* to feed whooper swans, greylag geese, mallards and eider ducks – in June and July there are a lot of cute ducklings around too. Just watch out for pushy seagulls trying to muscle in.

3 Visit the Museums

Iceland's most engaging museums for children are the Reykjavík's Settlement Exhibition, where they can see remains of a Viking longhouse;

the Saga Centre at Hvolsvöllur, full of swords and dioramas; Borgarnes Settlement Centre, showcasing spooky re-creations of Egil's Saga; and Húsavík Whale Museum, with its skeletons and marine mammal displays.

4 Eat a Hot Dog

Not exactly a cultural high point, but eating a *pylsur* (hot dog) from Bæjarins Bestu wagon in central Reykjavík is a rite of passage for young Icelanders, who form long queues outside this unpretentious mobile stand. The reason? The hot dogs taste great – though you might want to hold the onions. 🔞 *Map L2*
• *Tryggvagata, 101 Reykjavík*

5 Visit Reykjavík Harbour

Reykjavík has a busy harbour, with all types of colourful fishing boats and trawlers sailing in and out or hauled up on slipways for repairs. Look in the waters and you might also see jellyfish. Snack along nearby Geirsgata at either Búllan café *(see p43)* for burgers, or at Fish & Chips *(see p43)* on Tryggvagata. 🔞 *Map K1*

6 Go Horse Riding

Short and stocky Icelandic horses are even-tempered, making them child-friendly and a good choice for first timers. Most of the riding schools are very flexible with their schedules and duration of rides and cater especially to children *(see p50).*

Swimming pool, Laugardalur

Botanical Gardens, Reykjavík

7 Picnic at Reykjavík Botanical Gardens

A pleasant place for a family outing and picnic, just a short way from downtown Reykjavík (see p73). There is plenty of soft grass, ducks and geese wandering about, and – in summer at least – beds of colourful endemic flowers. Don't miss the small zoo, full of native mammals and birds.

8 Enjoy Whale-Watching

There is a good chance of seeing minke and humpback whales, orca, sperm whales and even blue whales as exciting rarities. Húsavík (see p94) is the best place for whale-watching.

9 Hunt for Trolls

Trolls, the mean, frightening, mischief-making giants, are said to inhabit several places across Iceland. They turn to stone if caught in the sunlight but their oddly-shaped, petrified forms can be seen (if you look hard enough) at many lava fields, mountain outcrops and sea stacks.

10 Go Beachcombing

Icelandic beaches are full of interesting flotsam and jetsam, from bird feathers and tumbled fragments of glass to oddly-shaped pebbles, tree trunks (which have floated here from Siberia) and even – if you are really lucky – whale bones.

Top 10 Icelandic Folktales

1 Eyvindur and Halla
Iceland's most famous medieval outlaw, who, along with his wife, Halla, survived 20 years on the run.

2 Viking Treasure at Skógafoss
Legend has it that a Viking named Þrasi hid his hoarded gold under Skógafoss.

3 The Beast of Hvalfjörður
This evil, red-headed whale terrorized Iceland's west coast until it was lured into a trap.

4 Ormurinn, the Lagarfljót Serpent
Iceland's elusive version of the Loch Ness Monster is said to inhabit Lögurinn Lake near Egilsstaðir.

5 Berþór
A friendly giant who lived at Bláfell, near Geysir, and died around 1000.

6 The Love-struck Shepherd
A favourite tale about a young man who waded across the River Hvítá to propose to a shepherdess.

7 Sæmundur the Wise
Founder of an 11th-century ecclesiastical school, who frequently took on and always defeated the Devil.

8 The Origin of Óxarár Falls
Said to be created around AD 930 when River Óxará at Þingvellir was diverted.

9 Were-Seals
Seals are thought to sometimes adopt human form, especially ones that swim close to shore.

10 Snorri
The wily thief Snorri escaped pursuit inside a small cave at Þórsmörk – it is near the bus stop.

Left **Hiking in Skaftafell** Right **Golf in Reykjavík**

Outdoor Activities

1 Hiking
Nothing gets you closer to Iceland's raw, natural landscape than hiking across it, following established trails ranging from an hour to a week. The pick of these are at Landmannalaugar, Jökulsárgljúfur, Skaftafell and Þórsmörk, where you can navigate grassy meadows with wildflowers, lava fields, black-sand deserts and icefields. ✦ Hiking organizations: www.fi.is, www.utivist.is

2 Swimming
Just about every Icelandic town has an outdoor geothermal swimming pool heated to 28°C (82°F), always with accompanying "hot pot" tubs at 34–38°C (93–100°F), and sometimes with saunas and water slides.

3 Horse Riding
Iceland's specific breed of horses arrived with the Vikings. Though lacking the size and speed of Arab horses, they have a unique gliding gait, called "tölt", used for moving softly over the rough terrain. Many riding schools and farms offer excursions.
✦ www.eldhestar.is, www.ishestar.is

4 Fishing
Recreational deep-sea angling is in its infancy here and most people fly fish for trout, salmon or charr (see pp64–5). A permit is essential: those for trout and charr are easy to find on the spot, but for salmon you need to apply in advance. ✦ www.angling.is/en

5 River Rafting
What Iceland's rivers lack in size they more than make up for in drama, tearing through narrow volcanic gorges, forming lively rapids. Two of the longest – the Þjórsá and the Hvítá – are accessible for white water rafting, with trips during the summer. ✦ www.arcticrafting.is, www.rafting.is

6 Snowmobiling
Snowmobiling or skidooing is an expensive but exhilarating way to tear across snowfields and glaciers at 40 kmph (25 mph). The best place to try it is at Skálafellsjökull, an outrunner of Vatnajökull. ✦ www.glacierjeeps.is

7 Jeep Touring
The harsh Interior – a spread of rough lava fields, gigantic icecaps and gravel plains braided by glacial rivers – is navigable only by high-clearance 4WDs. Public buses fit the bill and many private operators offer tours in off-road jeeps. ✦ www.glacierjeeps.is

Jeep crossing a stream in the Highlands

Preceding pages **Kayaking with a glacial backdrop**

8 Skiing and Snowboarding

There are established winter skiing and snowboarding venues around Reykjavík, Akureyri, Hlíðarfjall and in the West Fjords, complete with bunkhouses, ski lifts and graded runs. The most accessible is Bláfjöll, outside Reykjavík and the summer slopes at west Snæfellsjökull, with winter cross-country opportunities around Mývatn.
⊗ *www.skidasvaedi.is (Icelandic only)*

Skiing in Arnarstapi

9 Scuba Diving

There is only one area to scuba dive in Iceland – Silfra and other spots around Þingvallavatn. Silfra is rated as one of the best freshwater sites in the world, with crystal-clear, pale blue water and submerged lava formations as the main draws.
⊗ *Map C5 • www.dive.is*

10 Golf

Iceland's first golf clubs were founded in the 1930s, but recent years have seen an explosion of interest in the sport. There are currently over 50 courses, ranging from quirky 9-holers to internationally recognized 18-hole greens. Events include Akureyri's Arctic Open and the Volcano Open in Heimaey island *(see pp36–7)*.

Top 10 Places to Bathe and Swim

1 The Blue Lagoon

Surreal blue water, steam and black lava boulders feature at this ultimate bathing hot spot *(see pp10–11)*.

2 Laugardalur

Reykjavík's best public pool, complete with separate children's play pool and a steam room *(see p73)*.

3 Borgarnes

The town's swimming pool has exceptional views from the water's edge. ⊗ *Map B4 • Open 6:30am–9pm Mon–Fri, 9am–6pm Sat & Sun • Adm*

4 Landmannalaugar

Natural hot springs surrounded by lava walls and orange and grey rhyolite mountains *(see pp24–5)*.

5 Jarðböðin

Mývatn's answer to the Blue Lagoon, set up on a hillside among live volcanic scenery *(see p17)*.

6 Selárdalslaug

Tiny public pool near Vopnafjörður, beside the fast-flowing green waters of the Selá river. ⊗ *Map G2 • Open 10am–10pm daily*

7 Krossneslaug

Unforgettable hot springs and bathing pool in the north, near Norðurfjörður *(see p89)*.

8 Víti

The geothermally heated crater lake of Mount Askja *(see p17)* has sulphurous and milky coloured water. ⊗ *Map F3*

9 Grettislaug

Remote natural hot tub in the northwest, bathing place of Viking outlaw Grettir *(see p93)*.

10 Laugarvatn

Huge outdoor pool at the National School for Sports near Geysir. ⊗ *Map C5 • Open 10am–9pm Mon–Fri, 10am–6pm Sat & Sun • Adm*

Left **Eider duck, Vígur** Centre **Exhibit of basalt columns, Viðey** Right **Ptarmigan, Hrísey**

Offshore Islands

1 Viðey

Key historical figures have settled on this flat speck of land just off Reykjavík, amongst them the country's last Catholic bishop, Jón Arason, and sheriff Skúli Magnússon, who built Iceland's first stone house here in 1755. Today it is a stage for the circular Lennon Imagine Peace Tower and the night-time light show. ✒ *Map P5 • Daily ferries from Reykjavík • www.elding.is*

2 Lundey

There are plenty of places called Lundey around Iceland – the name means "Puffin Island" – but this is the closest spot to Reykjavík where you can actually see the bird in question, at least while they are nesting between April and August. You cannot land here, but cruises circle Lundey daily in summer. ✒ *Map P5 • Cruises from Reykjavík • www.elding.is*

3 Vigur

Out in the West Fjords, this remote, elongated islet makes a great half-day trip from Ísafjörður to see Arctic terns, puffins and especially eider ducks, whose warm, insulating down is commercially gathered for stuffing duvets and jackets. Only discarded chest feathers are collected and the birds are not harmed. ✒ *Map B2 • Daily ferry from Ísafjörður mid-Jun–late Aug • www.vesturferdir.is*

4 Hrísey

Up on the north coast near Akureyri, this island is famous for the colossal number of wild, but completely tame, ptarmigans that live here. Though common all over Iceland these birds can be rare in some years, so this is where to come if you have been unable to see them elsewhere. ✒ *Map E2 • Daily ferry from Árskógssandur • www.akureyri.is/hrisey/english*

5 Grímsey

Iceland's northernmost point and the only part actually crossed by the Arctic Circle – meaning the sun really does not set here for a few days either

Picturesque view of Hrísey

"ey" at the end of a word means "island".

Sleepy island of Flatey

side of 21 June and does not rise at all in late December. The island's cliffs are full of seabirds. A great day-trip destination. ⊗ *Map E1 • Ferry from Dalvík Mon, Wed, Fri at 9am; many flights a week from Akureyri • www.grimsey.is/english*

Papey

Papey (Monks' Island) is named after the Christian hermits who are believed to have been living here when the Vikings arrived in Iceland. Today the 2 sq km (1 sq mile) island, rising just 60 m (197 ft) out of the sea, is home to thousands of puffins, a few sheep and the smallest church in the country. ⊗ *Map H4 • Daily ferry from Djúpivogur Jun–Aug*

Flatey

Although hard to believe, this sleepy island half way across Breiðafjörður between Snæfellsnes and the West Fjords, housed an important 12th century monastery. Later it became famous for the Flateyjarbók, an illuminated medieval manuscript featuring the *Greenland Saga*, now kept in Reykjavík's Culture House. The island's east forms a reserve for nesting seabirds. ⊗ *Map E2 • Daily ferry from Stykkishólmur–Brjánslækur • www.saeferdir.is*

Heimaey

This 3-km- (2-mile-) long island off the south coast has enough birds, volcanoes, Viking history and walks to occupy you for a couple of sunny days. The town of the same name occupies the north end of the island and is famous for being nearly annihilated during a volcanic eruption in 1973. ⊗ *Map C6 • Daily ferry Herjólfur from Þorlákshöfn, flights from Reykjavík and Bakki • www.eimskip.com*

Eldey

About 15 km (9 miles) off Iceland's southwesternmost tip, Eldey's distinctive, rocky, sheer-sided cliffs rise 77 m (250 ft) straight out of the Atlantic. The top forms a level platform, home to Europe's largest gannet colony. Sadly, this is also where the last known pair of great auks were killed in 1844. ⊗ *Map B5*

Surtsey

Surtsey dramatically popped out of the waves during an underwater volcanic eruption southwest of Heimaey in 1963. Following erosion over the years, the island's size is now around 1.5 km (1 mile) across. Scientists are studying Surtsey to see how plants and animals colonize new lands, and being a special UNESCO reserve, this island is off-limits. ⊗ *Map C6*

People playing accordions at the Culture Night in Reykjavík

🔟 Festivals

1 Menningarnótt
One night in mid-August is designated Culture Night and downtown Reykjavík is closed to traffic as stages are set up, performers throng the streets and fireworks explode over the city. The entertainment is mainly amateur but well-known groups also participate at times.

2 Kvikmyndahátíð
A selection of the year's best in World Cinema gets a screening at the Icelandic Film Festival in late September, with events all around town. Look out for retrospectives of Icelandic masterpieces such as *Djöflaeyjan (Devil's Island)*, *101 Reykjavík* and *Sódóma Reykjavík* – the last a definite cult classic. ✪ *www.riff.is*

3 Reykjavík Arts Festival
This two-week showcase of concerts, operas, dances and theatre has been held every mid-May since 1970. Drawing local and international talent, it is organized at various venues, including the National Gallery, Nordic House and some churches, with spin-off events around Iceland through the summer. ✪ *www.listahatid.is*

4 Djasshátíð – Reykjavík Jazz Festival
The latest in jazz and blues come to Reykjavík for the last two weeks of August for this superb festival. There is always a smattering of international stars but the surprise is the quality and abundance of local talent. Do not miss the "Guitar Party" event. ✪ *www.myspace.com/reykjavikjazzfestival*

5 Fiskisúpudagurinn Dalvík
Early August sees Dalvík, the nondescript fishing village near Akureyri, draw the crowds with its "Fish Soup Day", a sort of eccentric, friendly social event that Iceland should be famous for. Apart from outdoor seafood buffets, look for homes displaying flaming torches – a sign that free fish soup is available. ✪ *Map E2*

6 Myrkir Músíkdagar
Held in February during odd-numbered years, the "Dark Music Days" festival brightens up Reykjavík's winter gloom with workshops and almost exclusively Icelandic contemporary music performances ranging from avant garde to opera. ✪ *www.listir.is/myrkir/English.html*

Giant puppet at Reykjavík Arts Festival

Gay Pride festival, Reykjavík

7 Gay Pride
Held annually since 1999, Reykjavík's Gay Pride festival goes from strength to strength, though the August timetable is asking a bit from the weather and rain is not unknown during the Saturday parade, which starts at Hlemmur bus station and winds through the downtown. ◈ www.gaypride.is

8 Þjóðhátíð Vestmannaeyjar
Westman Island Festival is not for the faint-hearted: camping for 4 days in August in a sodden volcano crater, serenaded by an unending line-up of Icelandic rock at maximum decibels and getting drunk enough to try skinny-dipping in the sea along with thousands of others. ◈ www.dalurinn.is

9 Kirkjubæjarklaustur Chamber Music Festival
The Kirkjubæjarklaustur Chamber Music Festival, held on the first weekend in August, showcases international talent among south Iceland's largest lava fields. It also provides a chance to explore small-town Iceland. ◈ Map E5

10 Síldarævintýri
Every August the small north coast town of Siglufjörður, once the North Atlantic's busiest herring port, holds a music festival known as the Herring Adventure in honour of the fish. It includes everything from traditional folk singers to Sigur Rós. ◈ Map D2

Top 10 Icelandic Musicians

1 Björk
This singer is Iceland's best-known musical export, though nowhere near as popular at home as abroad.

2 Sigur Rós
"Post-rock" band, Sigur Rós is a crossover between pop, classical and folk music and has absolutely unique vocals.

3 KK
Folk guitarist Kristján Kristjánsson is Iceland's Arlo Guthrie, quite often teaming up with veteran Magnús Eiríksson.

4 Stefán Íslandi
Born in 1907, Stefan Íslandi performed as an opera tenor in the US until his death in 1994.

5 Sigrún Hjálmtýsdóttir
A leading opera soprano and jazz singer, Sigrún Hjálmtýsdóttir has performed with José Careras and Placido Domingo.

6 Kristinn Sigmundsson
Massive operatic bass, Sigmundsson is well suited to playing Mephistopheles in Berlioz' Faust.

7 Mugison
Iceland's version of fusion-delta blues, this slide guitarist from West Fjords, Mugison, has an astounding voice.

8 Emiliana Torrini
Part Icelandic, part Italian, sweet-voiced singer Torrini is the first Icelander to top the German music charts.

9 Bubbi Morthens
Morthens is a mix of punk, Bruce Springsteen and Johnny Cash – minus the hair.

10 Kristinn Árnason
Brilliant classical guitarist, Árnason effortlessly manages the crossover into rock.

Left **A campsite** Centre **Svartifoss signage** Right **Eyjafjallajökull icecap**

🔟 Hiking Trails

1 Laugavegur
This stunning 4-day hike runs from Landmannalaugar, past hot springs and obsidian massifs, to the snowbound Hrafntinnusker Plateau, descending steeply to the green valley around Álftvatn. After many glacial rivers, a grey gravel desert at the foot of the Mýrdalsjökull icecap and canyons along Markarfljót, the trail ends in Þórsmörk's woodland *(see p25)*.

2 Fimmvörðuháls
An overnight trek from Skógar to Þórsmörk can be done separately or as an extension to Laugavegur. From Skógar, climb the steps to the top of the waterfall and follow the river upstream to cross the pass between Eyjafjallajökull and Mýrdalsjökull icecaps, descending to Þórsmörk. ◈ *Map D6 • Summer buses to Skógar and Þórsmörk. • Trail: open mid Jun–Sep; www.utivist.is*

3 Esja
Esja's 914-m- (2,999-ft-) high plateau rises unmistakably above the bay north of Reykjavík. Its snow-streaked slopes appear to mutate with the changing light – the colours shift from deep brown to pale blue. A return hike from the Mógilsá forestry station takes about four hours. ◈ *Map Q5*

4 Þingvellir
Þingvellir's mossy valley floor is criss-crossed by easy hiking trails of 1- to 3-hour durations.

One of the Þingvellir trails

Stick to marked paths, as vegetated lava flows conceal deep fissures. There are good views along the valley beside abandoned farm buildings at Skógarkot. ◈ *Map C5 • Daily buses from Reykjavik*

5 Svartifoss
Skaftafell National Park's most beautiful feature, Svartifoss (Black Falls), are located on an easy hiking trail atop Skaftafell Plateau. From the car park near Bölti guesthouse follow signposts for 10 minutes to the falls that drop into a 30-m (98-ft) gully *(see pp18–19)*.

6 Ásbyrgi
The top of this huge, curved cliff-face makes an excellent vantage point for admiring the north of Jökulsárgljúfur National Park. From the park headquarters, follow footpaths for 5 km (3 miles) through woodland to the top of Ásbyrgi *(see pp18–19)*.

Always carry food and water when hiking in Iceland.

7 Heiðmörk Park
A 28 sq km (11 sq mile) spread of lava, woodlands and picnic sites on the edge of Reykjavík city, with easy walking paths looping through it. Extend an excursion here by making a 3-hour circuit of the adjacent lake Elliðavatn, to view a variety of Iceland's flora. ✪ Map Q6

8 Hveragerði
The steamy hills and valleys immediately north of Hveragerði make for a good half-day hike from town, with hot springs along the way – bring a towel. There is a pegged path but be prepared for boggy ground, a couple of river crossings and unpredictable boiling vents. ✪ Map C5

9 Arnarstapi to Hellnar
The short coastal walk between the two small villages offers great seascapes and views of Snæfellsjökull's white cone. On the way look out for the statue of Bárður Snæfellsás and nesting Arctic terns. ✪ Map A1

10 Þórsmörk
This beautiful highland valley, with a braided glacial river, is overlooked by Mýrdalsjökull. Carry a map for the many day walks, as few trails are marked. ✪ Map D6 • Daily summer buses from Reykjavík • Only accessible May–Sep

View of Mýrdalsjökull

Top 10 Icelandic Wildflowers

1 Mountain Avens (Holtasóley)
Iceland's national flower, whose small fleshy leaves and yellow-centred white petals stand about 7 cm (3 in) high.

2 Arctic River Beauty (Eyrarós)
Late-flowering plant with distinctive symmetrical, pointed red petals and long leaves.

3 Moss Campion (Lambagras)
Spongy clumps of this bright pink flower brighten up the muddy, shaley slopes.

4 Wild Pansy (Prenningarfjóla)
Beautiful little plant with violet and yellow petals, common locally and abundant in June.

5 Bladder Campion (Holurt)
White flower found in small spreads, with a lilac-pink sack behind the petals.

6 Wild Thyme (Blóðberg)
Tiny, ground-hugging plant with deep red or purple flowers and distinct thyme smell.

7 Wood Cranesbill (Blágresi)
Widespread plant with geranium-like leaves and purple, five-petal flowers; favours woodland edges and reaches 30 cm (12 in) or more.

8 Butterwort (Lyfjagras)
Small, solitary plant with hanging blue flowers and cross-shaped leaves at ground level.

9 Northern Green Orchid (Friggjargras)
Easily overlooked in the grass, but look for pointed, leaves and little white flowers.

10 Purple Saxifrage (Vetrarblóm)
Widespread but very early-flowering, ground-hugging plant with little pink blooms.

Left **Steam vent at Námaskarð** Right **The Blue Lagoon**

Hot Springs and Geysers

Geysir
Now just a flooded crater at the top of a mound, Geysir once set the benchmark for erupting hot spouts worldwide until its subterranean vents became clogged with debris. A big earthquake in 2008 might have cleared some of them: new bubbling and hissing are the first signs of action for decades *(see pp12–13)*.

Jarðböðin Nature Baths
This mineral-rich natural spa uses its dramatic location on a steaming volcanic ridge overlooking Lake Mývatn to good effect. Take a look across the road too, where people have dug pits in the hot soil, covered them with metal lids, and use them as ovens for baking bread – and cooking sheep heads *(see p17)*.

Jarðböðin nature baths

The Blue Lagoon
Only Icelanders could turn the outflow from a geothermal power station into the country's premier tourist attraction. At the Blue Lagoon they have done a superb job, even if the first thing you see is people emerging from the milky-blue water with their faces covered in the fine white silt which is also sold as a beauty product *(see pp10–11)*.

Deildartunguhver
Water emerging at 97°C (207°F) at Deildartunguhver, Europe's largest hot spring, fills the skies with steam near the historic hamlet of Reykholt in west Iceland. There's no bathing pool here – the water is pumped straight to the coastal towns of Borgarnes and Akranes – but the violently spluttering vent is impressive. Ⓢ *Map C4*

Landmannalaugar
Popular with Icelanders and tourists alike, Landmannalaugar is the country's finest natural bathing pool – you just can't beat the feeling of soaking away in the hot stream here as a wall of lava towers overhead and fractured orange mountains frame the distance. No other part of the Interior is so wild, yet so accessible *(see pp24–5)*.

Strokkur
Geysir's stand-in, Strokkur *(see pp12–13)* is far more reliable too, erupting 10 times in an

Left **Strokkur** Right **Hveravellir**

hour – even at its peak, Geysir often lay quiet for days at a time. Strokkur is the largest continually active geyser in Iceland (and the one featured in most photographs), reaching impressive heights on a good day.

Seltún

Down on the Reykjanes Peninsula near Reykjavík, there was a decent geyser at Seltún in Krýsuvík, until the entire spring exploded in 1999, leaving behind a grey, bubbling pool. But smaller hot springs still seep out of the hills above, making for an interesting half-hour walk – do not leave the marked paths. ◈ *Map B5*

Námaskarð

This hillside east of Lake Mývatn, dotted with roaring steam vents and coloured mud pools, does a great job of demonstrating how raw and powerful nature can be *(see p17)*. The setting, with a lonely, sulphur-rich orange plain stretching away to the south, only adds to the impression.

Hveravellir

Famous hot spring on the interior Kjölur Route, it was once used by the 17th-century outlaw Eyvindur for warmth and to cook stolen sheep. A great spot to pause during the rough, 5-hour ride from Gullfoss to Akureyri and enjoy a soak in the cooler spa pool alongside. ◈ *Map D4*
• *Summer buses from Reykjavík and Akureyri* • *Bus schedules: www.bsi.is*

Hengill

Popular hiking area west of Hveragerði with hot springs and steam vents. Many of them are being diverted for geothermal energy projects – power plants and miles of silver coloured pipes for Reykjavík's water and electricity are visible nearby. ◈ *Map R6*

Left **Settlement Exhibition** Centre **Reykjavík Art Museum** Right **Ásmundur Sveinsson Museum**

🔟 Museums in Reykjavík

1 Listasafn Íslands (National Gallery)

A core collection of works by seminal Icelandic artists such as Ásgrímur Jónsson, contrasting with avant-garde installations by the likes of Hfrankell Sigurðsson and Krístján Guðmundsson. The gallery showcases regular archaeological and historical exhibitions. It is one of the main venues for the annual Reykjavík Arts Festival in June (see p71).

2 Þjóðminjasafn Íslands (National Museum)

An absorbing exploration of Iceland's history and culture, beginning with evidence of the earliest visitors (Roman coins found along the south coast), past Viking graves, carved doors, medieval church sculptures and 19th-century clothing, winding up with contemporary pop music and genetic research into the national family tree (see p72).

National Museum

3 Listasafn Reykjavíkur (Reykjavík Art Museum)

There is an exhibition by young Icelandic artists here, but the museum's backbone is work by Erró, born in western Iceland in 1932 and now living in France. Amongst sculptures, paintings and drawings, the most striking pieces are Erró's fantastic, multi-coloured collages depicting mythical figures in a blur of heroic activity. 🗺 Map L2
• Hafnarhús, Tryggvagata 17 • 590 1200
• Open 10am–5pm Sat–Wed, 10am–10pm Thu • www.artmuseum.is

4 Landnámssýningin (Settlement Exhibition)

The centrepiece to this excellent subterranean museum is the oval foundation wall of a Viking long-house, dated AD 871 with a distinctive underlying layer of vol-canic ash. Holographic dioramas and artifacts, including wooden farm implements and corroded axes, bring it all to life. Look for sacrificial cow bones among the foundations (see p71).

5 Einar Jónsson Sculpture Museum

Einar Jónsson's monumental pieces owe a good deal to the early 20th-century nationalist movements across Europe, with heroic marble figures in dramatic, iconic arrangements. One of the favourites is St George resting on the crucifix of his sword, holding his shield aloft, with the dragon, coiling behind (see p74).

 Many museums are closed on Mondays.

6 Sigurjón Ólafsson Sculpture Museum

Located along the foreshore, this gallery was founded by the artist's widow. It displays Sigurjón's modernist, abstract works in timber, stone and metal, ranging from smoothly-contoured sculptures to giant installations looking like totem poles made out of scrap iron and driftwood *(see p74)*.

Sigurjón Ólafsson Sculpture Museum

7 Gerðarsafn

This gallery concentrates on modern and contemporary artists with an eclectic range of styles and tastes and features a collection of work by Gerður Helgadóttir (1928–1975). Check the website for current exhibitions. ◎ Map Q5
• Hamraborg 4, 200 Kópavogur • 570 0442
• Buses from Lækjartorg or Hlemmur to Hamraborg • Open 11am–5pm Tue–Sun
• www.gerdarsafn.is

8 Sjóminjasafn (Seafarer's Museum)

The museum at Reykjavík's old harbour tries to convey a flavour of life on the ocean. Pick of the exhibits are the tiny, dangerous shallow-draft fishing boat (in use until the 1960s) and Ódinn, a coastguard vessel in dock outside. ◎ Map K1 • Grandagarður 8, 101 Reykjavík • 517 9400
• Open 1 Jun–15 Sep 11am–5pm daily, 16 Sep–30 May 11am–5pm Tue–Fri, 1–5pm Sat–Sun • Adm
• www.sjominjasafn.is

9 Árbæjarsafn

A former farm has now been converted into an open-air museum of old buildings, farm machinery and period artifacts. The best permanent exhibit is the turf-roofed timber house from the early 20th century. Regular events, when the machinery is fired up and domestic animals wander around, bring the place to life. ◎ Map P6
• Kistuhyl 4, Árbær • 411 6300 • Bus 12, 19 or 24 from Hlemmur & Lækjartorg • Open Jun–Aug: 10am–5pm daily, Sep–May: 1–2pm Mon, Wed, Fri or by appointment
• Adm (Fri free) • www.arbaejarsafn.is

10 Ásmundur Sveinsson Sculpture Museum

The building is an attraction in itself, but the real pleasure is walking around the sculpture garden outside, full of Ásmundur's powerful depiction of themes from history and folklore, influenced by cubism and African tribal art. Inside are smaller pieces in a variety of media *(see p74)*.

Left **Herring Era Museum** Right **A display at the Icelandic Emigration Centre**

Museums Around Iceland

1 Borgarnes Settlement Centre

The museum is in two halves and its entry price includes audio guides. Upstairs, Iceland's settlement is covered in detail, from a pneumatic longship prow to impressions of how the islands looked then with more trees and no sheep. Downstairs, *Egil's Saga* is brought to life with depictions of key scenes from this violent tale *(see p79)*.

2 Icelandic Emigration Centre

The museum's lonely setting on the north coast, gives some idea of the feelings endured by the thousands of 19th-century Icelanders who left for Canada following a catastrophic series of harsh winters and volcanic eruptions. ◈ *Map D2 • Hofsós • 453 7935 • Buses in summer • Open Jun–Aug: 11am–6pm daily • Adm • www.hofsos.is*

3 Skógar Museum

Fascinating collection of artifacts documenting over 1,000 years of life here. There is a brass ring off a Viking treasure chest, traditional turf buildings, a Bible from 1584 (Iceland's first printed book), a fishing boat and clothing. ◈ *Map D6 • Skógar • 487 8845 • Buses from Reykjavík and Höfn • Open May–Sep:10am– 5pm, Oct–Apr: 11am–4pm daily • Adm • www.skogasafn.is*

Settlement Centre

4 Herring Era Museum

A sleepy place today, Siglufjörður was – until fish stocks declined during the 1960s – the busiest herring port in the country, its harbour crammed with boats. The museum documents those hectic times in photos, models and dioramas, including photographs of the armies of "herring girls" who cleaned and salted the catches. ◈ *Map D2 • Snorragata 10, Siglufjörður • 467 1604 • Buses in summer • Open Jun–Aug: 10am–6pm & Sep–May: 1–5pm daily • Adm • www.sild.is*

5 Keldur

The oldest surviving turf-roofed house in the country, Keldur was built in Viking times and continually inhabited until the 1940s. The medieval historian Snorri Sturluson was raised at a nearby farm by his foster father. Look for original wooden beams, flagstoned floor, stone firepit and the hidden escape tunnel.

Skógar Museum

Nearby Gunnarssteinn was the site of a Viking skirmish. ⊛ Map D5 • Keldur, near Hvolsvöllur • Open 15 Jun–5 Aug: 10am–5pm daily • Adm

6 Húsavík Whale Museum
Overlooking Húsavík harbour, where whaling boats are now used for whale-watching tours, this museum uses videos, relics and whole minke and humpback skeletons to provide information on whales. It is essential viewing before heading seawards to see them. ⊛ Map E2 • Hafnarstétt 1, Húsavík • 414 2800 • Open Jun–Aug: 9am–7pm, May & Sep: 10am–5pm daily • Adm • www.whalemuseum.is

Exhibit at the Húsavík Whale Museum

7 Phallalogical Museum
Definitely the most eccentric museum in the country, dedicated to collecting together penises from every species of Icelandic mammal, which are displayed dried, preserved in jars, or stuffed and mounted on the walls. Former visitors have even sent in plaster casts of their own worthy organs to complete the exhibition. ⊛ Map E2 • Hédinsbraut 3, Húsavík • 868 7966 • Open 20 May–10 Sep: noon–6pm daily • Adm • www.phallus.is

8 Langabúð
The oldest wooden building on Djúpivogur harbour, Langabúð was built as a warehouse in 1790 and is now a cultural centre, folk museum and a memorial to the local artist Ríkarður Jónsson (1888–1977). He taught drawing and sculpture and his works are on display here. It also has a coffee shop. ⊛ Map G4 • Djúpivogur • 478 8220 • Buses run between Höfn and Egilsstaðir in the summer • Open Jun–Sep: 10am–6pm daily • Adm

9 Turnhús
Ísafjörður was settled in the 1580s and later became a busy port for saltfish. The town has a museum located in the 18th-century Turnhús (the towerhouse was a lookout post) which documents those times. Photographs show that the town centre has changed little since the early 20th century. ⊛ Map B2 • Turnhús, Suðurgata, Ísafjörður • 896 3291 • Open 15 May–15 Sep: 9am–6pm • Adm • www.nedsti.is

10 Viking World
The modern, glass-sided museum just outside Keflavík houses the Íslendingur, a full-scale reproduction of a wooden Viking longship unearthed in Norway in the 1880s. Íslendingur was built by captain Gunnar Marel Eggertsson, who sailed in it to New York in 2000 to celebrate the millennium of the Viking discovery of North America. ⊛ Map B5 • Víkingabraut 1, 260, Reykjanesbær • 422 2000 • Open 11am–6pm daily • Adm • www.vikingaheimar.com

Left **Brown trout** Right **Norðura**

Fishing Spots

1 Elliðaár
Despite a hydro power dam, each year around 1,500 salmon are hauled out of this 10-km- (6-mile-) long river, which runs right through Reykjavík's suburbs. This is the country's only salmon river offering half-day permits, making it slightly more affordable than most. Ⓢ *Map P5 • 568 6050 • www.svfr.is*

2 Laxá í Kjós
About an hour's drive from Reykjavík, this 25-km- (16-mile-) long river comprises waterfall pools, rapids and long, flat, stretches – in short, perfect conditions for salmon. Lodge owners offer permits, guides and 4WDs. Ⓢ *Map Q6 • 534 2130 • jthj@islandia.is*

3 Laxá í Aðaldal
Misleadingly known for its salmon fishing – *laxá* means "salmon river" – this is a classic brown trout river, flowing 60 km (37 miles) north from Lake Mývatn to the sea through some gorgeous scenery. Over 4,000 fish, weighing up to 5 kg (10 lb) are caught here each year. Ⓢ *Map E2 • 557 6100 • veidi@laxamyvatn.is*

4 Hítará
The 30 km- (19-mile-) long river has an annual bag of 350 salmon, a few trout and charr. It is popular due to its accessible, wild location and an eccentric, old lodge nearby. Book in advance. Ⓢ *Map B4 • 568 6050 • www.svfr.is*

5 Vatnasvæði Lýsu
A series of interconnected lakes and streams on the Snæfellsnes Peninsula, and one of the few single locations in the country where you have a good chance of catching trout, charr and salmon. It is unreliable, so less expensive. Ⓢ *Map B4 • 557 6100*

6 Norðurá
This is an expensive, prestigous salmon river with fickle water levels and an annual catch upwards of 1,500 fish. Although the Norðurá is 65-km- (40-mile-) long, only 12 people can fish here at a time. There is a lodge in the area for a stay and meals. Ⓢ *Map C3 • 568 6050 • www.svfr.is*

7 Vatnsdalsá
One of north Iceland's better salmon rivers with about 20 km (12 miles) of suitable terrain along its 40-km- (25-mile-) length, made famous by British author

Angling at Hítará

 For more on fishing permits See pp123, 126

and one-time owner John Ashley-Cooper. The annual haul of 1,000 fish is not huge, but they tend to weigh above average. Salmon over 5 kg (10 lb) are released back for spawning numbers.
◈ *Map D3* • *551 2112 or 897 1498*

Elliðavatn
This lake just southeast of Reykjavík is the source of the Elliðaár river, with a nature reserve on the eastern side and a riding track along the shore. Look out for the brown trout.
◈ *Map Q6* • *For permits: 568 6050*

Fishing for trout

Hópið
An estuary lake spread over 30 sq km (19 sq miles), it is best known for charr and trout, which are netted by locals through the spring and autumn; anglers get sole access from mid-June until mid-August. ◈ *Map C3* • *466 4000, 898 4006* • *www.veidikortid.is*

Ytri-Rangá
Near Hella in south Iceland, this is the richest salmon river in the country thanks to a recent smolt release programme – a staggering 14,315 were landed in 2008, with an average weight of over 4 kg (8 lb). You need to plan the trip in advance. ◈ *Map C5* • *557 6100* • *www.fishiceland.com*

Top 10 Icelandic Fish

1 Cod
The backbone of Iceland's traditional fishing industry, the cod used to appear on the Icelandic coat of arms.

2 Haddock
A popular deep water fish around 1-m (3-ft) long, with big spawning grounds in the southwestern Icelandic waters.

3 Halibut
Huge, bottom-dwelling flatfish weighing up to 200 kg (440 lb), with both eyes on the same side of its body.

4 Ocean Perch
Large-eyed deepwater fish with bright red scales; tastes excellent when grilled whole.

5 Ocean Catfish
Abundantly-fanged and with sweet, firm flesh, the ocean catfish is also known as the wolf fish. It is unrelated to the fresh-water catfish.

6 Atlantic Salmon
Freshly-caught Atlantic salmon is some of the best in the world and tastes even better smoked

7 Brown Trout
Excellent sport and eating fish, the brown trout is mainly confined to freshwater rivers and lakes in Iceland.

8 Arctic Charr
Another fine fish for eating, it is often hooked in winter by fishing through holes in the frozen lakes.

9 Monkfish
Ghastly looking, globular, flattened sea fish with a huge semi-circular mouth and sweet, delicious meat.

10 Lobster
Also known as the langoustine or Norway lobster, it is another favourite on Reykjavík's restaurant menus.

Left **Detail of Þingeyrarkirkja** Centre **Viðimýri's turf chapel** Right **Church at Grund**

Churches

Dómkirkjan
This small, stone and corrugated-iron Lutheran cathedral was built between 1788 and 1796 just as Reykjavík, previously just a collection of farm buildings and warehouses, began to coalesce into Iceland's first town. The interior shows off the building's unadorned but beautiful and simple proportions to best effect. ⊗ *Map L2*
• *Austurvöllur Square, Reykjavík* • *520 9700* • *Open 10am–4:30pm Mon–Fri*

Landakotskirkja
Iceland's Catholic faith was fiercely stomped out in 1550, so it is not surprising that this cathedral dates back to only 1929. Perhaps not to offend Protestant feelings, the building is functional and plain in the extreme, and it is only the font at the entrance and statue of the Virgin Mary that gives the denomination away.
⊗ *Map K2* • *Túngata 15, Reykjavík*
• *552 5388* • *www.catholica.is*

Skálholtskirkja
Functioning as Iceland's first bishopric from 1056 until 1801, Skálholt became an important educational centre and, at one point, was the country's largest settlement. Check out the memorial outside dedicated to Iceland's last Catholic bishop, Jón Arason and the 13th-century tomb of bishop Páll Jónsson. Music concerts are also held at the cathedral.
⊗ *Map C5* • *Skálholt, Biskupstungur*
• *486 8870* • *Daily bus from Selfoss; tours from Reykjavík* • *www.skalholt.is*

Hóladómkirkja
Seat of Iceland's second bishopric since the 12th century, this remote, attractive cathedral dates to the 1760s, though some of the sculptures inside – and the ornate altarpieces – are centuries older. The country's first printing press was founded here by bishop Jón Arason in 1530, who is buried in a small adjacent chapel. ⊗ *Map D2* • *Hólar í Hjaltadal*
• *895 9850* • *Regular buses Jun–Sep* • *www.kirkjam. holadomkirkja.is*

Bænahús at Núpsstaður
Wedged below tall cliffs, Núpsstaður is a collection of antique turf farm buildings, including Bænahús church, which was once considered Iceland's remotest holding despite its

Plain exterior of Landakotskirkja, Reykjavík

proximity to the coast. Until the 1850s the nearest harbours were at distant Eyrarbakki and Djúpivogur, and stock had to be transported inland via the daunting highland roads. ◈ Map E5
• Núpsstaður, near Kirkjubæjarklaustur

Hallgrímskirkja

Vast in scale as it stands proudly over Reykjavík, Hallgrímskirkja is not a cathedral, though it is Iceland's biggest church. Designed in 1945, construction was undertaken by a family firm of just two people and the building work dragged on, incredibly, until 1986. The exterior was again renovated in 2009 (see p72).

Þingeyrarkirkja

This beautiful stone church up in northern Iceland stands close to a Viking assembly site and the presumed location of the country's first monastery. Þingeyrarkirkja's medieval alabaster altar was carved in England. The ceiling of the church is painted blue and studded with hundreds of gold stars that create a gorgeous effect (see p96).

Víðimýri

The 19th-century tiny turf chapel at Víðimýri is one of only six surviving in Iceland, with an attractive timber interior. Check out the walls, weatherproofed by stacking thick slices of earth in a "herring

Inside Hallgrímskirkja, Reykjavík

bone" pattern, and the pretty summertime flowers growing on the grassy roof. ◈ Map D3
• Víðimýri, Skagafjörður
• 453 6173 • Open Jun–Aug: 9am–6pm daily

Strandakirkja

Standing beyond a seashore hamlet at the eastern end of the Reykjanes Peninsula, Strandakirkja is a picture-perfect 19th-century church, painted pale blue and built on a firm base of square-cut lava blocks. According to legend, it was funded by grateful sailors who made it ashore at this very spot during a storm. ◈ Map C5
• Selvogur, near Þorlákshöfn

Grund

An extremely odd church, at least for Iceland, with an onion-domed cupola topping its wooden tower and Romanesque mini-spires. Though the building is fairly recent – built by farmer Magnús Siggurðsson in 1905 to serve the entire valley – Grund was once a wealthy holding. The treasures of the church include a 15th-century chalice, kept at the National Museum in Reykjavík.
◈ Map E3 • Grund, Eyjarfjörður

AROUND ICELAND

ICELAND'S TOP 10

Left **Laugardalur swimming pool** Right **Botanical Gardens**

Reykjavík

REYKJAVÍK CAPITAL AREA COVERS THE CITY CENTRE, *plus a handful of satellite suburbs. The city's tiny core focuses on a historic precinct of lanes near the old harbour, easily covered on foot in a day. While the municipal buildings are made of stone or concrete – practical protection against the fierce winter winds – most of the area is residential, comprising old wooden houses, weatherproofed in brightly coloured corrugated iron. Here you will find most of the shops, cafés, restaurants and famously raucous nightclubs, alongside museums and galleries. A distinctive landmark is Öskjuhlíð hill, with a scattering of more distant sights and modern suburbs.*

Höfði house

🔟 Sights

1. Historic Midtown and Harbour
2. Landnámssýningin
3. Þjóðmenningarhúsið
4. Listasafn Íslands
5. Þjóðminjasafn Íslands
6. Hallgrímskirkja
7. Kjarvalsstaðir Art Museum
8. Höfði house
9. Perlan
10. Laugardalur Park and Recreation Area

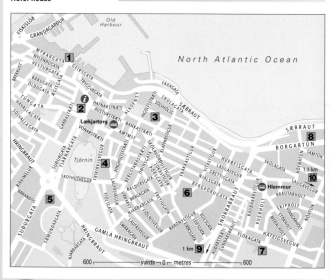

Preceding pages **Strokkur geysir**

1 Historic Midtown and Harbour

Reykjavík's historic midtown occupies the site of Iceland's first Viking settlement (now being excavated near Austurvöllur Square) and the city's oldest standing building (an 18th-century wooden storehouse on

Buildings in the historic midtown area

the adjacent Lækjatorg Square). Off Austurvöllur, a statue of Jón Sigurðsson *(see pp30–31)* faces the 1881 Parliament Building, which replaced the Alþing's original home at Þingvellir. Just north, check out the busy old harbour and the whaling fleet. ✆ *Map K1*

2 Landnámssýningin (Settlement Exhibition)

This impressive exhibition comprises the in-situ remains of a large Viking-age longhouse, possibly belonging to Iceland's first official settler, Norwegian Ingólfur Arnarson, who sailed to Iceland around AD 870. A visit here will surround you in a factual past; there are virtually no other contemporary remains in such good condition. Its location under the capital's streets makes it even more incredible. ✆ *Map K2 • Aðalstræti 16 • 411 6370 • Open 10am–5pm daily • Adm • www.reykjavik071.is*

3 Þjóðmenningarhúsið (Culture House)

Stored in Denmark for centuries, Iceland's precious medieval manuscripts were returned to the country in the 1970s and are now displayed in the old National Library. Look for the *Codex Regius* containing the "Edda", the main source for Norse mythology; the *Flateyjarbók*, which includes the only known copy of the *Greenland Saga*, documenting Leifur Eiríksson's discovery of "Vínland" (North America) and the huge compendium of sagas known as the *Möðruvallabók*. There is also an excellent account of the composition and history of the manuscripts. ✆ *Map L2 • Hverfisgata 15 • 545 1400 • Open 11am–5pm daily • Adm (Wed free) • On-site café (weekends); guided tours available • www.thjodmenning.is*

4 Listasafn Íslands (National Gallery)

The nation's main collection of art is housed in a former warehouse where blocks of ice, cut from the nearby lake, were once stored. The gallery concentrates on early 20th-century Icelandic painters. There is a continual rotation of the estimated 10,000 works and regular space is dedicated to contemporary and traditional art, so there should be something of interest even if you have visited before. ✆ *Map L3 • Fríkirkjuvegur 7 • 515 9600 • Open 11am–5pm; closed Mon • www.listasafn.is*

Viking era manuscripts, Culture House

The Settlement of Reykjavík

When Ingólfur Arnarson first saw Iceland on his voyage from Norway in AD 870, he threw overboard his valuable wooden seat-posts and vowed to settle wherever they washed up. They were finally found in a broad, fertile, steamy inlet on the island's southwest, which Ingólfur named Reykjavík ("Smoky Bay").

5 Þjóðminjasafn Íslands (National Museum)

This museum documents Iceland's history and culture from the earliest evidence of settlement to the present. A floor is devoted to the early period – DNA testing is used to trace Viking heritage. Whether it is Viking grave goods, medieval statues or Björk's musical career, the chances are you will find something interesting over the two floors. ✪ Map K3 • Suðurgata 41 • 530 2200 • Open 16 Sep–30 Apr: 11am–5pm Tue–Sun; 1 May–15 Sep: 10am–5pm daily • Adm (Wed free) • www.natmus.is/

6 Hallgrímskirkja

The largest in Iceland, this 73-m- (240-ft-) high church took 40 years to build and resembles a volcanic formation, covered in hexagonal pillars. The interior is unadorned but hearing the organ is an experience; it is a stunning instrument with 5,000 pipes. Take the lift to the tower for views over Reykjavík's colourful rooftops and Leifur Eiríksson's statue. ✪ Map M3 • Skólavörðuholti • 510 1000 • Open 9am–5pm daily • Cathedral free; tower adm • www.hallgrimskirkja.is

Hallgrímskirkja's organ

7 Kjarvalsstaðir Art Museum

Jóhannes Kjarval (1885–1972), born in a tiny village in the northeast, studied painting in Europe. On returning to Iceland he began incorporating the landscapes into his brightly-coloured paintings. Though considered Iceland's greatest artist, his work often controversially blended folklore, Christianity and paganism. Apart from his works, this museum also exhibits contemporary Icelandic as well as foreign art. ✪ Map N4 • Flókagata 24 • 517 1290 • Open 10am–5pm daily • Guided tours by arrangement • www.listasafnreykjavikur.is

8 Höfði house

Originally the French Consulate, this whitewashed wood house, believed to be haunted, dates back to 1909. Winston Churchill stayed here in 1941, but its main claim to fame is that the presidents of Russia and US, Mikhail Gorbachev and Ronald Reagan, ended the Cold War here in 1986. Don't miss the modern *Solar Voyager* sculpture, representing Viking travels, on the seafront nearby. ✪ Map P2 • Borgartún

Exhibition at the National Museum

9 Perlan

Just south of the city centre is Perlan ("the Pearl") the mirrored glass dome atop Öskjuhlið hill. This imaginative building, with six cylindrical water tanks converted into a tourist attraction, has great views and a renowned restaurant *(see p40)*. One tank is the Saga Museum, which brings alive the Viking period with wax dioramas. Ⓢ *Map M6 • Öskjuhlið • Bus 18 from Hlemmur • Saga Museum: 511 1517; open 1 Apr–30 Sep: 10am–6pm daily; 1 Oct–31 Mar: noon–5pm weekends; adm; audio guides; www.sagamuseum.is • Building entry free*

10 Laugardalur Park and Recreation Area

East of the centre, Laugardalur Park is a great spot to join local families relaxing. The Botanical Gardens also have a zoo full of native species and a duck pond. You can skate in winters at the adjacent sports centre or visit year-round the naturally-heated 50-m- (164-ft-) long outdoor pool, with three smaller play pools and hot tubs. Ⓢ *Map R4 • Laugardalur • Bus 14 from Hlemmur • Pool: 553 4039, open 1 Apr–1 Sep: 6:30am–10:30pm Mon–Fri, 8am–10pm Sat & Sun, 8am–8pm Sat & Sun in winter • Park free; activities adm*

Perlan's entrance

A Day in Reykjavík

Morning

🕙 Kick off the day the way many Icelanders do – by having a swim at central **Sundhöllin** indoor pool before work. After a coffee at **Kaffitár** on Bankastræti, head for the **National Museum** and get a solid grounding in Icelandic history, though don't burn out by trying to cover it all on a single trip. Amble down to get some fresh air and feed the birds at **Tjörnin** *(see p74)*, before ducking inside **City Hall** for a look at their giant relief map or to catch a lunch-time concert. Sit out on the grass at **Austurvöllur Square** *(see p71)*, to admire the humble Reykjavík Cathedral, Art Deco Hótel Borg and Parliament House. Then spend half an hour among Viking remains at the excellent **Settlement Exhibition** *(see p71)* located nearby.

Afternoon

Reboot your energy levels with a leisurely bowl of Icelandic lamb soup at **Café Paris** *(see p76)*, then shop for jewellery, clothes or souvenirs along **Laugavegur**. Head uphill, past a street of colourful houses on Klapparstígur, to take in the cityscape from the top of **Hallsgrímskirkja**. If you have room for another museum, soak up some Saga-Age ambience at the **Culture House** *(see p71)*. Walk north to the seafront and the **Solar Voyager** sculpture, before strolling along the seafront looking for seals. Plan an assault of the city's nightclubs – **NASA** *(see p44)*, right in the city centre, is the place to start.

Left **Ráðhúsið (City Hall) beside Tjörnin lake** Right **View of Viðey island across Stóra tjörn lake**

TOP10 Best of the Rest

1 Noræna húsið
The Modernist Nordic House, designed by Finnish architect Alvar Aalto, hosts exhibitions and concerts. Its library is devoted to Nordic culture. ✪ *Map K4 • Sturlugata 5 • 551 7030 • Open 9am–5pm Mon–Fri, noon–5pm Sat & Sun • www.nordice.is*

2 Ráðhúsið Reykjavíkur
The glass-and-steel City Hall houses the mayor´s office. There is a huge table-top relief map of Iceland in the foyer. ✪ *Map K2 • Tjarnagata 11 • 411 1000 • Open 8am–7pm Mon–Fri, noon–6pm Sat & Sun • Summer lunchtime concerts • www.rvk.is*

3 Alþingishúsið
This 19th-century rectangular building houses the world's oldest National Parliament, which was founded at Þingvellir in AD 930 and relocated here in 1881. ✪ *Map L2 • Austurvöllur • 563 0500 • Open 8am–7pm Mon–Fri • www.althingi.is*

4 Tjörnin
Locals bring their children to feed the ducks, geese and swans at this stone-edged pond in the city centre. ✪ *Map K3*

5 Sigurjón Ólafsson Sculpture Museum
Once the studio of artist Sigurjón Ólafsson (1908–1982), this Nordic style seafront building displays his sculptures. Concerts are held here in summer. ✪ *Map Q1 • Laugarnestangi 70 • Buses 12 & 15 • 553 2906 • Open Feb–May, Nov: 2–5pm Sat & Sun, Jun–Oct: 2–5pm Tue–Sun • www.LSO.is*

6 Ásmundur Sveinsson Sculpture Museum
With Mediterranean and African influence, this building is as inter-esting as the displayed works of the renowned sculptor. ✪ *Map Q4 • Sigtun • 590 1200 • Open May–Sep: 10am–4pm daily; Oct–April: 1–4pm*

7 Hafnarfjörður
Reykjavík's seaside suburb is home to good restaurants and an annual Viking festival. ✪ *Map P6 • Bus 1 from Hamraborg • www.hafnarfjordur.is; www.fjorukrain.is*

8 Viðey
Just off Reykjavík, this grassy isle boasts Iceland's oldest stone building (now a restaurant), thou-sands of seabirds and the Lennon Imagine Peace Tower. ✪ *Map P5 • 15 May–30 Sep: 8 ferries daily from Skarfabakka, and 1 daily from Reykjavík´s Old Harbour • www.videy.com*

9 Einar Jónsson Sculpture Museum
Iceland's first modern sculptor, Einar Jónsson's (1874–1954) 300 marble statues are displayed here against vivid backdrops. ✪ *Map M3 • Eiríksgata • 551 3797 • Open June–15 Sep: 2–5pm Tue–Sun; 16 Sep–30 Nov, 1 Feb–31 May: 2–5pm Sat & Sun • Adm • www.skulptur.is*

10 Öskjuhlíð
Perlan *(see p73)* is the biggest draw of this wooded hill-side, but walking tracks also lead to a sandy bathing beach and a thermal pool nearby. ✪ *Map M6*

Most museums offer student and pensioner discounts.

Left **Fríða Frænka** Right **Display at Ostabúðin Skólavörðustíg**

Places to Shop

Kirsuberjatréð
This unique store, run by a women's cooperative, offers distinctly Icelandic garments, fish-skin accessories, glassware, jewellery and gift items. ◈ *Map L2* • *Vesturgata 4* • *562 8990* • *www.kirs.is*

Fríða Frænka
Search for unusual gifts in the old corrugated iron house, stuffed with antique furniture and quirky knick-knacks. ◈ *Map L2* • *Vesturgata 3* • *551 4730*

Thorvaldsens Bazar
In business for over a century, this charity shop specializes in hand-made jumpers, local woodcarvings, clothing and silver jewellery. ◈ *Map L2* • *Austurstræti 4* • *551 3509* • *www.thorvaldsens.is*

Mál og menning
Excellent bookshop with a big range of maps – from road atlases to detailed hiking ones – English books on Iceland, stationery and T-shirts. Has a good café upstairs. ◈ *Map L2* • *Laugavegur 18* • *515 2500*

12 Tónar
Music CDs and vinyl, with an eclectic inventory of local artists covering jazz, classical and pop. ◈ *Map L3* • *Skólavörðustíg 15* • *511 5656*

Kraum
Local designers display and sell their clothes and accessories here. Look for attractive silver and black lava jewellery. ◈ *Map L2* • *Aðalstræti 10* • *517 7797* • *www.kraum.is*

Sævar Karl
Though Iceland may not be the best place for a bargain suit, head here if you need to surround yourself with elite threads by the likes of Joop!, Prada and Armani. ◈ *Map L2* • *Bankstræti 7* • *551 3470* • *www.saevarkarl.is*

Frank Úlfar Michelsen
Great old-style watchmaker, with a workshop full of half-repaired pre-digital timepieces. Sells Rolexes and other classic wrist watches. ◈ *Map L2* • *Laugavegur 15* • *511 1900*

Ostabúðin Skólavörðustíg
Gourmet deli specializing in cheese with a renowned, relatively inexpensive snack bar known for its "new Icelandic" take on food – excellent raspberry vinaigrette and fish steaks. ◈ *Map L3* • *Skólavörðustígur 8* • *562 2772*

Kolaportið Flea Market
Join locals and spend a couple of hours sifting through acres of household junk here and you might uncover unexpectedly stylish designer clothing. Good home-grown veggies too. ◈ *Map L2* • *Tryggvagata 19* • *562 5030* • *Open 11am–5pm Saturday & Sunday.*

Left **Hornið** Right **Café Paris**

Bars, Cafés and Pubs

1 Café Paris
Popular meeting place for locals and tourists. Try the sandwiches or crepes for lunch. Sit outside in good weather.
⊗ *Map L2 • Austurstræti 14 • 551 1020*

2 Cultura Café
Popular expat hangout with good live music on weekends, theme nights and reasonably priced international food.
⊗ *Map L2 • Hverfisgata 18 • 511 1310 • Open 3pm–1am Mon–Fri, 5pm–1am Sat–Sun*

3 Vegamót
Restaurant-bar with a great patio, busy at lunchtime and after office hours. Good for people watching over a drink, or to sample the Asian-influenced menu.
⊗ *Map L3 • Vegamótstigur 4 • 511 3040*

4 Íslenski Barinn
The Icelandic Bar serves traditional Icelandic delicacies and beer. Waffles and coffee are served every Sunday and there is live music on Thursday, Friday and Saturday. ⊗ *Map L2 • Pósthússtræti 9 • 578 2020*

5 Grái Kötturinn
This trendy basement café serves huge, superb breakfasts. Popular place to get coffee after a night out. ⊗ *Map L2 • Hverfisgata 16a • 551 1544 • Open 7am–late*

6 Hornið
In business since 1979, this family-run, cosy Italian pizzeria is rumoured to have served the country's first espressos. Their fresh seafood pastas are superb.
⊗ *Map L2 • Hafnarstræti 15 • 551 3340*

7 Café Rosenberg
Classic folk, jazz and blues bar offers simple meals. Open for decades although the original building burned down in 2007.
⊗ *Map M3 • Klapparstígur 25 • 551 2442*

8 Celtic Cross
High-ceiling Irish bar, serves Guiness, but the crowds pile in for the exceptional vibe – they have been known to have two bands playing at the same time.
⊗ *Map L2 • Hverfisgata 26 • 511 3240*

9 Sandholt
This family bakery serves tasty breads, Danish pastries, quiches, chocolates, sandwiches and superb coffee. ⊗ *Map M3 • Laugavegur 36 • 551 3524*

10 Mokka
This no frills café – said to be Reykjavík's oldest – spearheaded the caffeine culture.
⊗ *Map L3 • Skólavörðustíg 3a • 552 1174*

Around Iceland – Reykjavík

Set menus have to be ordered by the whole table.

Price Categories

For a three course meal for one (without alcohol), with taxes and extra charges.

k	under ISK3,000
kk	ISK3,000–5,000
kkk	ISK5,000–7,000
kkkk	ISK7,000–9,000
kkkkk	over ISK9,000

Left **Fjalakötturinn**

🔟 Restaurants

1 Við Tjörnina
Smart restaurant (with house speciality seafood dishes) overlooking Tjörnin – guests even get a free bag of bread to feed the ducks. ◈ *Map L3 • Tomplarasundi 3 • 551 8666 • kkk*

2 Domo
French-Japanese influenced seafood, quality sushi and fruity desserts served in a stylish setting. ◈ *Map L3 • Þingholtsstræti 5 • 552 5588 • kkkk*

3 Lækjarbrekka
This famous eatery, housed in an old storehouse in the city centre, is full of period furnishings. Top-notch traditional seafood. ◈ *Map L2 • Bankastræti 2 • 551 4430 • 11am–11pm daily • kkkkk*

4 Humarhúsið
This 19th-century building is one of the best places for fresh lobster. Try their "four-course mystery menu". ◈ *Map L2 • Amtmannstig 1 • 561 3303 • kkkkk*

5 Caruso
Period furnishings and an Italian menu make Caruso an elegant but not a formal place to dine – they even serve pizzas. Bar on second floor. ◈ *Map L2 • Þingholtstræti 1 • 562 7335 • kkk*

6 Fjalakötturinn
The finest home-grown lamb and salmon compete for your approval with the décor and service. A Viking longhouse was excavated here. ◈ *Map K2 • Hótel Reykjavík, Aðalstræti 16 • 514 6060 • kkkk*

7 Einar Ben
It has a limited menu – fish, beef or lamb – but it is probably the best meal you will have in Iceland. ◈ *Map K2 • Veltusundi 1 • 511 5090 • kkkk*

8 Restaurant Reykjavík
Known for its seafood, this beautiful old wooden warehouse overlooks Ingólfstorg. Try the delicious Portuguese-style cod or visit the adjacent Ice Bar. ◈ *K2 • Vesturgata 2 • 552 3030 • kkk*

9 Brauðbær
Friendly grill restaurant where you can get a tasty steak, burger, club sandwich and cold *snorrabrauð* dishes. Kids menu available. ◈ *Map L3 • Hótel Óðinsvé, Þórsgata 1 • 511 6200 • kkk*

10 O-Sushi
For raw seafood, check out this slick sushi restaurant done in greys, steel and pine. Dishes are colour-coded according to price. ◈ *Map L2 • Lækjargata 2a • 561 0562 • k*

Left **Wild horses, Hvalfjörður** Right **Búðir Hotel, Snæfellsnes Peninsula**

West Iceland and the Snæfellsnes Peninsula

Heading north from Reykjavík, the highway follows the weatherbeaten western coastline, famous for its stormy weather and good farmland. Beyond Hvalfjörður and the exceptional Glymur falls, Akranes reveals itself as a workaday town and, apart from a good museum, there's more cause to pause around atmospheric Borgarnes, once home to the notorious Viking Egill Skallagrímsson. The 13th-century historian, Snorri Sturluson, lived (and was murdered) just inland at Reykholt, close to an attractive set of waterfalls and more saga lore around Laxárdalur. Northwest of Borgarnes, the long Snæfellsnes Peninsula's coastline is dotted with tiny fishing villages and its tip graced by Snæfellsjökull, the conical icecap covering a dormant volcano.

Cultural Centre, Reykholt

🔟 Sights

1. Borgarnes Settlement Centre
2. Reykholt
3. Hraunfossar, Barnafoss and Kaldidalur
4. Stykkishólmur
5. Breiðafjörður and Flatey
6. Búðir
7. Snæfellsjökull National Park
8. Laxárdalur
9. Akranes
10. Hvalfjörður

1 Borgarnes Settlement Centre

Iceland's Settlement Period, the Landnám, began in AD 870 when the Viking settlers arrived and lasted until all free land had been occupied around AD 930. This museum explores the period, using archaeological finds and near-contemporary records of the first colonists. A section of the museum celebrates the life of the warrior-poet Egill Skallagrímsson, who was born in Borgarnes.
⊗ Map B4 • Brákarbraut 13-15, Borgarnes • 437 1600 • Daily buses from Reykjavík • Open Jun–Aug: 10am–7pm daily, Sep–May: 11am–5pm daily; restaurant: 11am–9pm daily • Adm • www.landnam.is

2 Reykholt

Set in the Reykholtsdalur Valley, the tiny hamlet of Reykholt belies its importance as the home of Snorri Sturluson (1179–1241), the historian who became tangled in Norway's bid to annex Iceland. Snorri was murdered by a rival who had the support of the Norwegian king, Hákon. He was trapped as he fled down a tunnel beneath his farmhouse. His tale is told at Snorrastofa, below Reykholt's church; his thermal bathing pool and restored remains of the tunnel are nearby. ⊗ Map C4 • Snorrastofa, Reykholt • 433 8000

Scene from Egil's Saga, Settlement Centre

• Open 1 May–30 Sep: 10am–6pm daily, 1 Oct–30 Apr: 10am–5pm Mon–Fri • Adm • www.snorrastofa.is

3 Hraunfossar, Barnafoss and Kaldidalur

About 15 km (9 miles) east up the valley from Reykholt along Route 518, contrasting twin waterfalls at Hraunfossar and Barnafoss – one a gentle cascade, the other a violent tumble – are worth a stop on the way to Kaldidalur, a stark valley between the icy peaks of Ok and Þórisjökull. The 70-km (44 mile) road, which follows routes 551, 550 and 52 to Þingvellir, is unsealed, though open in summer to ordinary vehicles driven with care (check conditions at www.vegagerdin.is), providing an easy taste of the interior. ⊗ Map C4

4 Stykkishólmur

This pleasant town has old wooden buildings recalling its 19th-century heyday as a herring port. Best of these is the Norska húsið, the Norwegian House, now a museum full of photographs. Stykkishólmur's pretty harbour is busy with fishing boats and the countryside is dotted with sites from the Eyrbyggja Saga. Don't miss the path through the Berserkjahraun lava field, said to have been cut by two berserkers in AD 982.
⊗ Map B3 • 438 1640 • Norska húsið: open 31 May–7 Sep: 11am–5pm daily • www.stykkishólmur.is

Harbour at Stykkishólmur, Snæfellsnes Peninsula

Church at Búðir

Breiðafjörður and Flatey

Breiðafjörður – the huge, wide bay separating the Snæfellsnes Peninsula from the West Fjords to the north – is thick with islands and rocky reefs, providing an ideal breeding ground for marine birds. From Stykkishólmur, you can explore the bay on a tour with Sæferðir (www.seatours.is), or go to Brjánslækur in the West Fjords via Breiðafjörður's largest island, Flatey, once home to an important monastery. For a taste of island life and bird-watching, stay at Flatey's tiny village (www.hotelflatey.is). **◊** *Map B3*

Búðir

Búðir is a minute place on Snæfellsnes' south coast, with just a church and a hotel. One can enjoy beautiful seascapes and views of Snæfellsjökull from here. The dark wooden church dates from 1703, its graveyard and boundaries encroached upon by the Buðahraun lavafield, said to be inhabited by creatures from local folklore. Despite its remote location, the romantic Hótel Búðir *(see p130)* is famous for being a favourite with Nobel Prize winning author Halldór Laxness. Don't miss the amazing black-sand beach. **◊** *Map A4*

Snæfellsjökull National Park

Based around an ice-capped volcano, this national park featured in the classic tale *Journey to the Centre of the Earth*. It extends over rough, vegetated lava fields to a coast-line rich in birdlife. Hiking, skiing or exploration of local villages are all possibilities, and you can easily circuit the park by car in a day *(see pp20-21)*.

Laxárdalur

This pretty valley along Route 59 is the setting for the *Laxdæla Saga*, Icelandic literature's great tragic love story. It tells of the beautiful Guðrún Ósvífursdóttir and her four husbands: the first she divorces but the

View of Snæfellsnes Peninsula

rest perish due to witchcraft, feuding and drowning while she becomes a nun. Only place-names from that time survive, namely the church at Hjarðarholt, and farmsteads at Goddastaðir and Höskuldsstaðir. ◈ Map C3

Akranes

Akranes, Iceland's oldest fishing port, is a good place to experience a down-to-earth, gritty Icelandic town. Fishing is still the main industry and the harbour and processing factory survive alongside the less romantic National Cement Works. The town is famous for its sports club, Íþróttabandalag Akraness, whose football team has won the national games 18 times. The engaging Museum Centre *(see p82)* provides a good reason to visit, though it is a 10-km (6-mile) detour off the highway. ◈ Map B5

Fishing boat in Akranes Museum Centre

Hvalfjörður

Most people use the tunnel under the bay to bypass the 30-km- (19-mile-) deep Hvalfjörður, but miss some classic scenery, including Glymur *(see p32)*, the isle's highest waterfall. Hvalfjörður means "whale fjord", after the number of whales once seen here. It was also a US naval base during World War II and the red barracks have now been turned into holiday homes. ◈ Map C4

A Day in the West

Morning

Head north from Reykjavík around windswept Kjalarnes, where the road is pinched between the sea and the domineering Esja Plateau. Avoid the 5-km- (3-mile-) long cross-fjord tunnel and follow Route 47 around **Hvalfjörður**. At the head of the fjord, take the 4-km (3-mile) gravel road inland to where the magnificent **Glymur** waterfall cascades down the 200-m- (656-ft-) high cliffs. Continue around Hvalfjörður to rejoin Route 1 and continue to **Borgarnes**. Spend an hour at the **Settlement Centre**, *(see p79)* delving into the lives of Iceland's Viking pioneers. Don't miss out on the spooky dioramas downstairs, retelling the tale of Egil's Saga. Have a quick lunch at the good-value café here.

Afternoon

Make **Deildartunguhver**, Europe's largest thermal spring *(see p58)*, the first stop of the afternoon followed by a further historical halt at **Reykholt**, taking in the Heimskringla Museum, the church and old geothermal bathing pool. From here, follow Route 518 to **Hraunfossar and Barnafoss** *(see p32)*, the latter the setting for a tragic tale of two children who drowned in the rapids here while trying to cross over a lava bridge. Both falls are small but very attractive, especially for keen photographers. At this point you can retrace your route or – though this is an adventurous, summer-only option – follow gravel tracks south via **Kaldidalur** to **Þingvellir** *(see pp8–9)* and head back to Reykjavík.

Left **Old fishing boat outside the Akranes Museum Centre** Right **Cave opening, Surtshellir**

TOP 10 Best of the Rest

1 Borg á Mýrum
Site of Egill Skallagrímsson's home, but nothing contemporary survives. The statue, *Sonatorrek* (Lament for my Dead Sons), is named after his poem. ⊗ Map B4

2 Eiríksstaðir
The reconstructed longhouse of Viking Eirík Þorvaldsson, known as Eirik the Red, and his son Leifur, who explored Greenland and North America. ⊗ Map C3 • Eiríksstaðir, Haukadal, 371 Búðardalur • 434 1118 • Open Jun–Sep: 9am–6pm daily • Adm • www.eiriksstadir.is

3 Gamla Pakkhúsið
This warehouse, built in 1844, houses the tourist office, a café and a folk museum. Photographs and fishing memorabilia outline the town's history. ⊗ Map A3 • Ólafsbraut, Ólafsvík • 433 6930 • Open Jun–Aug, by appointment • Adm

4 Kerlingarfjall
Route 56 to Stykkishólmur crosses Kerlingarfjall, a mountain said to be haunted by the ghost of a female troll, who turned to stone on her way back from a fishing expedition. ⊗ Map B3

5 Húsafell
Picturesque spread of woodland and meadows east of Reykholt, with an old church, open-air geothermal swimming pool and petrol station serving the scattered community of summer houses used by holidaymakers. ⊗ Map C4

6 Surtshellir
Large subterranean cave near Húsafell, named after giant Surtur. Later used by outlaws, who also hid stolen livestock here. ⊗ Map C4

7 Akranes Museum Centre
Four museums in one centre – Folk, Mineral, Sports and Land Survey Museums. ⊗ Map B5 • Að Görðum, Akranes • 431 5566 • Open Jun–Aug: 10am–5pm Sep–May: 1–5pm daily • Adm • www.museum.is

8 Berserkjahraun
The *Eyrbyggja Saga* tells how a berserker was promised a local man's daughter if he cleared a path through this lava field, but was murdered once he completed the task. ⊗ Map B3

9 Stykkishólmur church
Shaped like an abstract ship, music recitals are held here from June to August. ⊗ Map B3 • Open 10am–5pm daily • Charge for recitals

10 Glanni
A pretty cascade over black lava on the Norðurá salmon river near Bifröst. You can see salmon as they head upstream. ⊗ Map C4

Price Categories

For a three course meal for one (without alcohol), with taxes and extra charges.

k	under ISK3,000
kk	ISK3,000–5,000
kkk	ISK5,000–7,000
kkkk	ISK7,000–9,000
kkkkk	over ISK9,000

Left **Restaurant at Hótel Hamar**

Places to Eat

1 Hótel Búðir
Probably western Iceland's finest diner, it focuses on fresh lamb and seafood dishes served in a smart setting. It is cheaper than similar Reykjavik venues *(see p130)*. ✆ Map A4 • kkkk

2 Hótel Hamar
Less formal than the Búðir but with a similar menu and exceptional vistas out over the sea. The attached bar has a balcony with more views *(see p130)*. ✆ Map B4 • kkkk

3 Settlement Centre
Great for an inexpensive meal – either the catch of the day, the lunch special of soup, salad and bread, or filling pasta dish. Interesting vegetarian options too. ✆ Map B4 • Brákarbraut 13-15, Borgarnes • 437 1600 • Open summer: 10am–9pm daily • kk

4 Hyrnan Snack Bar
Popular alternative to the ever-crowded Shell petrol station canteen, this is a place to grab a sandwich or a pizza in the adjacent shopping centre. ✆ Map B4 • Brúartorg, Borgarnes • k

5 Fosshótel Reykholt
The top place to eat in Reykholt, though in truth there's not much choice. The menu offers straightforward soups and grills; guests at the hotel also get to use the outdoor hot tubs. ✆ Map C4 • 320 Reykholt • 435 1260 • kkkk • www.fosshotel.is

6 Hótel Hellissandur
Within sight of Snæfellsnes' slopes, this hotel restaurant provides Icelandic staples such as fish of the day and burgers, excellent coffee and cakes. The bar is open until late. ✆ Map A3 • Klettisbúð 9, Hellissandur • 430 8600 • kkk • www.hotelhellissandur.is

7 Hótel Glymur
Smart retreat with an equally accomplished menu – carpaccio beef, pan-seared trout and homemade icecream. The café serves tasty snacks. Beautiful rural setting. ✆ Map C3 • Hvalfjörður • 430 3100 • kkk • www.glymurresort.com

8 Fjöruhúsið
Small café with good-value meals – especially famous for fish soup, coffee, home-made cakes and great harbour views. ✆ Map A4 • Hellnar, Snæfellsnes • 435 6844 • Open Jun–mid-Sep: 10am–10pm daily • k

9 Fimm Fiskar
Hearty, tasty pizzas, burgers and grills, plus a well-stocked bar await at this welcoming retreat near the Stykkishólmur harbour. ✆ Map B3 • Frúarstíg 1, Stykkishólmur • 436 1600 • Open May–mid-Sep • kk

10 Narfeyrarstofa
Similar menu to the nearby Fimm Fiskar but more inspired. The older wooden building with a tiny lounge and comfortable sofas gives it an edge. ✆ Map B3 • Aðalgata 3, Stykkishólmur • 438 1119 • From 11:30 am • kkk • www.narfeyrarstofa.is

Left **Dynjandi falls** Right **Church in Hrafnseyri**

The West Fjords

THERE IS IMMENSE GRANDEUR *in the high, flat-topped mountains, brilliant blue seas and rugged coastline of the West Fjords, located on the extreme northwest of Iceland. For the region's scattered communities, life has been tough given the minimal infrastructure outside Ísafjörður, the only sizeable town. Attractions are mostly strung along the Fjords' west coast between Látrabjarg bird cliffs and Ísafjörður. Though the eastern Strandir coast offers its own low-key beauty, all inland views are filled by snow-streaked plateaus. It is best to visit in summer when the roads are open: you can fly into Ísafjörður but from there you will need to drive further.*

Látrabjarg landscape

Sights

1. Flókalundur
2. Patreksfjörður
3. Rauðasandur
4. Látrabjarg Bird Cliffs
5. Hólmavik Museum of Sorcery and Witchcraft
6. Hrafnseyri
7. Ísafjörður
8. Súðavík Arctic Fox Centre
9. Norðurfjörður
10. Drangajökull

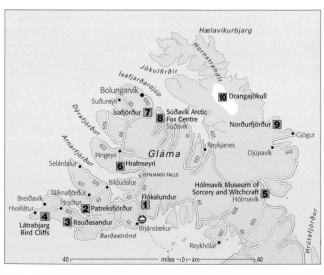

1 Flókalundur

Flókalundur ("Flóki's Wood") is a tiny south-coast community on Route 62, named after the Viking Flóki Vilgerðarson. He endured a harsh winter here around AD 860 and, and on climbing nearby Lónfell, he saw the fjord below choked with ice and gave "Ice Land" its name. The surrounding wetlands, dwarf forest and barren basalt highlands are now protected as the Vatnsfjörður National Park, which you can explore using Hótel Flókalundur *(see p91)* as a summertime base. The hotel also runs a small store, fuel pump, campsite and restaurant. ✪ *Map B2 • Vatnsfjörður National Park: http://english.ust.is*

2 Patreksfjörður

Named after St Patrick, this comparatively sizeable fishing village on Route 62 is where Iceland's trawling industry kicked off from in the early 20th century. Patreksfjörður is famous for attacks by Basque pirates during the early 17th century. It is also the last place to stock up with provisions and fuel if you are heading to the Látrabjarg bird cliffs or the fantastic beach at Breiðavík *(see p23)*, southwest across the fjord at the end of Route 62. ✪ *Map A2*

3 Rauðasandur

Seals are frequently seen at this cinnamon-coloured beach at

Rauðasandur Beach

the southwesternmost peninsula of West Fjords, along the unsealed Route 614. Arctic skuas nest on the grasslands behind the spit – don't go too close or you may get a sharp peck on the head. The stone ruins of Sjöundá farm lie 5 km (3 miles) to the east of the beach. Gunnarson's novel, *Svartfugl (Blackbird)* is based on a double murder that took place at the farm in 1802. A steep and slippery track leads to sea views from Skor's high cliffs. ✪ *Map A3*

4 Látrabjarg Bird Cliffs

Látrabjarg is among the most stirring sights of Iceland, with millions of seabirds crammed into the tall cliffs throughout the summer – the noise and stench are remarkable in itself. The dramatic landscape, empty beaches and isolated buildings evoke visions of the hardships of rural life. Local buses make day trips to Látrabjarg during the summer months *(see pp22–3)*.

A view of Patreksfjörður village

Timber from the Sea

Iceland has always been short of home-grown timber for building boats and houses, which from Viking times has placed great demand on driftwood. Fortunately, plenty washes up around the country, particularly along the West Fjords' pebbly Strandir Coast, whose beaches are often strewn with tree trunks which have floated in from Siberia.

Windmill on Vigur Island

5 Hólmavík Museum of Sorcery and Witchcraft

A shrimp port on the southeast coast, Hólmavík has a Museum of Sorcery and Witchcraft which draws on the district's reputation for the dark arts – during the 17th century 20 witches (only one was female) were burned at the stake. The museum has models, trinkets, an audio tour and a live demonstration of spell-casting. They run a "Sorcerer's Cottage" 40 km (25 miles) up the coast, a reconstruction of the 20th-century shepherd dwellings. ⊗ Map C2
• Höfðagata 8, 510 Hólmavík • 897 6525, 451 3525 • Open 1 June–15 Sep: 10am–6pm daily • Adm • www.galdrasyning.is

6 Hrafnseyri

Hrafnseyri – simply a church and turf farmhouse overlooking the sea at Arnarfjörður – is of great importance as it is the birthplace of Jón Sigurðsson

(1811–1879), whose campaign for Iceland's independence from Denmark saw the parliament restored and a self-governing constitution enacted. His birthday, 17 June, is celebrated as National Day. The farmhouse is now a museum. Don't miss the dramatic Dynjandi waterfalls, 15 km (9 miles) to the south. ⊗ Map B2
• 456 8260 • Open on request • Adm

7 Ísafjörður

The region's main town and the only one with an airport, Ísafjörður is a likeable place with narrow streets and old buildings. Chief among these is the Turnhús (see p63), overshadowed by the steep slopes of Kirkjubólsfjall. Across Ísafjarðardjúp straits the uninhabited Hornstrandir Peninsula offers the ultimate hiking challenge. Boats run out here and to little Vigur island (see p52), through the summer. ⊗ Map B2
• Tourist office: 450 8060, www.isafjordur.is

8 Súðavík Arctic Fox Centre

Originally the only mammal in Iceland was the Arctic fox, which probably drifted from Greenland on ice floes. Larger than the European fox, the Arctic fox has a dark blue summer coat (which turns white in winter) and lives on

Bust of Jon Sigurðsson at Hrafnseyri

ground-nesting birds such as ptarmigan. This centre, 20 km (12 miles) around the coast from Ísafjörður at Eyrardalur farm, explores the Arctic fox's biology and relationship with man. ✎ *Map B2*
• *Eyrardal, Súðavík* • *862 8219* • *www. arcticfoxcenter.com, www.melrakki.is*

Norðurfjörður

Just at the end of Route 648 up the east Strandir coast, Norðurfjörður is a small place, even for the West Fjords, but the scenery is stunning and makes the drive along loose gravel roads worthwhile. The town is backed by the 646-m- (2,125-ft-) high Krossnesfjall and looks out to sea across Norðurfjörður Bay, a lonely but romantic location. About 4 km (2 miles) around the coast lies Krossneslaug, a great beachside swimming pool, fed by a hot spring. ✎ *Map C2*

Drangajökull

The area's sole permanent icecap, Drangajökull is fairly remote, but makes a splendid sight on the top of a high plateau. During the 18th century it covered local farms but has now shrunk. The best close-up view is along the dead-end Route 635 to Kaldalónsjökull, a glacier descending off larger Drangajökull. It is an hour's walk from Kaldalón. ✎ *Map B2*

Drangajökull icecap, Hornstrandir

A Day in the West Fjords

Morning

🕐 Arriving at **Brjánslækur** by ferry from Stykkishólmur on the Snæfellsness Peninsula *(see pp78–81)*, drive north up Route 62 to **Flókalundur** *(see p87)*, fuel up and buy something for a picnic lunch here before turning on to Route 60. This good gravel road climbs up to the Dynjandisheiði Plateau and then drops abruptly to the coast at the stunning and noisy **Dynjandi** waterfall *(see p32)*, a great place to stretch your legs and spend an hour exploring the multi-level cascades (the lighting is best here in the evening). A grassy area at the foot of the falls makes a perfect spot for a picnic.

Afternoon

Leaving Dynjandi waterfalls, carry on around the bay to **Hrafnseyri**, birthplace of Jón Sigurðsson *(see p31)*, and drop in at the museum celebrating the life of this great Icelandic patriot. From here it is a further 65 km (40 miles) to **Ísafjörður** via Þingeyri, the West Fjords' oldest trading town, two mountain passes and a lengthy single-lane tunnel – there are passing bays inside, but traffic is never heavy. Once at Ísafjörður, track down your accommodation and then visit the **Maritime Museum** inside the antique **Turnhús** or simply stroll the handfull of streets down to the harbour, where you can usually spot marine ducks. The nearby **Faktorshús** *(see p91)* is an ideal place for a late afternoon coffee and cake.

Left **Traditional fishermen's houses at Ósvör Museum** Right **A view of Breiðavik Bay**

Best of the Rest

1 Pennugil
This narrow canyon on the Penná river is about a 30-minute walk from Flókalundur on a marked trail, with a bathable hot spring feeding it nearby. ✎ *Map B2*

2 Reiðskörð
Route 62 runs past this tall and fragmented volcanic dyke at Barðaströnd, the bay south of the West Fjords. ✎ *Map A3*

3 Brautarholt
Self-taught artist Samúel Jónsson (1884–1969) lived in this isolated valley at the end of Route 619, and created a bizarre range of sculptures and buildings.
✎ *Map A2 • Selárdalur, Arnarfjörður*

4 Skrúður
Set at the foot of a valley on Route 624, Iceland's oldest botanical garden was founded in 1909 by Reverend Sigtryggur Guðlaugsson. ✎ *Map A2 • Núpur*

5 Bolungarvík
This weatherbeaten fishing port is worth a trip to look at turf buildings and wooden fishing boats at the Ósvör Museum. The Natural History Museum showcases local stuffed birds. ✎ *Map B1 • Ósvör Museum: 892 1616, open by appointment; Natural History Museum: 456 7507, open 6 Jun–16 Aug 9am–noon & 1–5pm Mon–Fri, 1–5pm weekends*

6 Djúpavík
Wild and beautiful Djúpavík, halfway along Strandir's lonely coast, is dominated by a century-old shipwreck and a defunct herring processing factory. ✎ *Map C2*

7 Reykjanes
The hamlet of Reykjanes, a detour on Route 61 east from Ísafjörður, has a geothermal pool and sauna. ✎ *Map B2*

8 Kaldalón
Kaldalón ("Cold Lagoon") is fed by Drangajökull glacier *(see p89)*. It inspired local musician Sigvaldi Stefánsson (1881–1946) to call himself Kaldalóns. ✎ *Map B2*

9 Hælavíkurbjarg
This vertical, 258m- (847 ft-) high cliff between Hælavík and Hornvík islets, along with Látrabjarg and Hornbjarg, is one of the area's major bird colonies. ✎ *Map B1*

10 Hvallátur
Iceland's westernmost settlement comprises a farm and hotel at Breiðávík beach. It played a central role in the *Dhoon* shipwreck rescue *(see p23)*. ✎ *Map A2 • www.breidavik.is*

Price Categories

For a three course	**k** under ISK3,000
meal for one	**kk** ISK3,000–5,000
(without alcohol),	**kkk** ISK5,000–7,000
with taxes and	**kkkk** ISK7,000–9,000
extra charges.	**kkkkk** over ISK9,000

Left **Restaurant in Hótel Ísafjörður**

Places to Eat

1 Hótel Ísafjörður
This hotel's restaurant, Við Pollinn has a Nordic décor and offers tasty, local standbys such as the catch of the day, grilled lamb and seafood soup *(see p130)*. ✆ Map B2 • 456 3360 • kkkk

2 Faktorshús
A great old wooden building that once housed Ísafjörður's trading manager, is now a hotel and café serving snacks and cakes. The location in an old part of town adds atmosphere. ✆ Map B2 • Hæsti Kaupstaður, Ísafjörður • 899 0742 • k

3 Hamraborg Snack Bar
This DVD rental and fast-food place serves burgers, sandwiches, pizza and *pylsur* (hot dogs) with remoulade, onions and tomato sauce. ✆ Map B2 • Hafnarstræti 7, Ísafjörður • 456 3166 • k

4 Hótel Flókalundur
Small restaurant with aluminium chairs has a pricey evening menu with well-prepared seafood and game dishes. Better-value, set lunch specials. ✆ Map A2 • Vatnsfirði 451, Patreksfjörður • 456 2011 • Open 20 May–20 Sep • kkk • www.flokalundur.is

5 Hótel Laugarhóll
Pleasant hotel in a marvellous setting with a thermal pool and hiking trails within walking distance. Its excellent restaurant has set and à la carte menus. ✆ Map B3 • Klúka, Strandir, Bjarnarfjörður • 451 3380 • kkk • www.strandir.is

6 Hótel Djúpavík
Another friendly place in a fantastic location, the hotel is largely self-catering. Also offers breakfast and dinner by arrangement. ✆ Map C2 • Djúpavík, Strandir • 451 4037 • kkk • www.djupavik.com

7 Café Riis
The best restaurant on the Strandir coast, with pan-fried puffin breast, roast trout and lamb fillets served with panache. Also provides sandwiches, burgers, cakes and coffee. ✆ Map C2 • Hafnarbraut 39, Hólmavík • 451 3567 • kkk • www.caferiis.is

8 Hótel Bjarkalundur
If you are driving in or out of the West Fjords along Route 60, then the welcoming restaurant at the otherwise insignificant Hótel Bjarkalundur will be very welcome. ✆ Map B3 • Reykhólahreppi • 434 7762 • kkk • http://bjarkalundur.is

9 Hótel Flatey
Simple but well-prepared lamb and fish dishes at reasonable prices given the remote location on an island in the bay between Snæfellsnes and West Fjords. ✆ Map B3 • Flatey, Breiðafjörður • 422 7610 • kkk • www.hotelflatey.is

10 Þorpið
Good grill restaurant serving the usual fare, but the seafood is above average, which it should be given the town's great seafaring heritage. ✆ Map A2 • Aðalstræti 73, Patreksfjörður • 456 1295 • kk

Left **Boiling mud pool in the Hverir area, Lake Mývatn** Right **Hraun í Öxnadalur farm**

North Iceland

RICH IN HISTORY AND WILDLIFE *and with an amazing landscape, North Iceland could easily make for a week-long trip. There is the pleasant regional capital, Akureyri, with its fjord setting and old buildings; a glut of birds and volcanic attractions around Lake Mývatn; Húsavík's laid-back charm, unusual museums and whale-watching cruises; Jökulsárgljúfur's incredible gorge system and waterfalls; not to mention a wealth of antique farms, churches and saga sites, some of them – such as Hólar – central to Icelandic culture. Almost everything is located on or easy to reach from Route 1.*

Sights

1. Blönduós
2. Sauðárkrókur
3. Hraun í Öxnadalur
4. Dalvík
5. Akureyri
6. Hólar
7. Húsavík
8. Lake Mývatn
9. Jökulsárgljúfur
10. Dettifoss

Detail of the altar at Hólar Church

1 Blönduós

The most striking thing about this small riverside fishing port and regional service centre on Húnaflói Bay is its extraordinary church, consecrated in 1993, whose steeply sloping concrete walls echo the shape of the mountains nearby. The acoustics are good too, if you are lucky enough to catch the choir performing. Other attractions include trips to see seals and birdlife in the bay and 15 km (9 miles) west at Vatnsdalshólar, an expanse of strange mounds formed during an earthquake, site of Iceland's last execution in 1830. 🖾 *Map D2*

2 Sauðárkrókur

Approached from a lush valley, Sauðárkrókur's appeal comes from the tiny knot of atmospheric old buildings that surround the town "square", principally the church and Hótel Tindastóll (www.hoteltindastoll. com), which are said to be haunted. The coast here features in *Grettir's Saga*, including the sheer-sided Drangey island, where Grettir spent his last years as an outlaw; and Grettislaug, a marvelous seaside thermal bathing pool where he recovered after swimming over from the island in search of fresh embers to reignite his own fire. 🖾 *Map D2*
• *Drangey boat trips with Jón Eiríksson, 453 6310, 20 May–Aug, fagri@simnet.is*

Street in the old part of Sauðárkrókur

3 Hraun í Öxnadalur

This nondescript farm by the roadside in the deep, glacier-carved Ox Valley is famous as the birthplace of poet and biologist Jónas Hallgrímsson (1807–1845). Hallgrímsson's romantic verses extolling the landscape influenced the way Icelanders, most of whom then lived poor lives in rural turf buildings, began to perceive their country as glorious rather than embarrassing. He is one of the two people honoured with burial at Þingvellir Church *(see p8)*. 🖾 *Map E2*

4 Dalvík

Dalvík is a small port with an unusual Fish Soup Festival *(see p54)* and boats to Grímsey island *(see pp52–3)*, and also serves as a jump-off point for ferries to the ptarmigan-rich Hrísey island. The nearby Svarfaðadalur Valley is great for hiking. Though most of the set trails are lengthy, you can also spend just a couple of hours strolling or picking whortleberries during autumn. 🖾 *Map E2*

Around Iceland – North Iceland

Dalvík port with mountains in the background

Around Iceland – North Iceland

Grettir's Saga

Grettir's Saga recounts the life of Grettir Ásmundarson, a fierce warrior who performs great deeds in the service of others, but is haunted by a *draugur* or evil ghost. Grettir ends his life as an outlaw on Drangey island, where he is finally killed by his enemies.

Whale-watching, Húsavík

Akureyri

Iceland's largest settlement after Reykjavík with a population of over 17,000, Akureyri is a relaxed town with a pretty harbour and lots of shops, cafés and restaurants. Looming over everything is Akureyrarkirkja, the huge church, with excellent stained-glass windows (some brought from England's old Coventry cathedral) and some modern depictions of famous Icelanders. Do not miss the Botanical Gardens, where both native and imported plants thrive, or the Viking-age burial remains at the Akureyri Museum. ◈ *Map E2 • Tourist Info: www.visitakureyri.is; Akureyri Museum: Aðalstræti 58, 462 4162, www.akmus.is*

Hólar

More fully known as Hólar í Hjaltadal, this was once the largest settlement in northern Iceland thanks to the monastery and religious school founded in 1106 by bishop Jón Ögmundsson, which attracted scholars and monks from across Europe. These institutions survived the Reformation – which saw the execution of Hólar's last Catholic bishop, Jón Arason – and today the cathedral *(see p66)* and the college specializing in aquaculture, rural tourism and horse science are the sole buildings here. ◈ *Map D2 • Tourist office: 455 6333; open summer: 8am–10pm; booking@holar.is*

Húsavík

A delightful town overlooking the wide Skjálfandi Bay, Húsavík is Iceland's whale-watching capital, with several daily tours throughout summer. There is also the superb Whale Museum, the offbeat Phallalogical Museum *(see p63)* and an informative museum in the town library. The coast makes for some good walks along grassy headlands and little beaches from where you might see seals. ◈ *Map E2 • Whale watching tours: www.gentlegiants.is and www.northsailing.is*

Lake Mývatn

Whether you have come to Iceland to climb cinder cones, hike over steaming expanses of recently solidified lava, bathe in open-air geothermal pools, see hot mud pools, make a day-trip

Akureyrarkirkja (Akureyri Cathedral)

into the stark interior deserts or simply spend time bird-watching, you will find it all at Lake Mývatn. Although many sights are spread around the lakeshore, you will need a vehicle to reach the outlying attractions which include a flooded volcano crater known as "Hell" (see pp16–17).

9 Jökulsárgljúfur

Set in a northern segment of the massive Vatnajökull National Park (see pp18–19), this mighty canyon is excellent for hiking, following the top of the gorge or cutting across a land rich in flowers and birdlife. Sights along the way include striking red formations at Rauðhólar, twisted hexagonal granite columns at Hljóðaklettar, Hólmatungur's springs and Dettifoss (see p32). ◈ Map F2 • National Park: http://ust.is

10 Dettifoss

Part of the attraction of visiting this waterfall is the effort needed to get there, as the roads are rough gravel and open only for a few months each year. The eastern approach is easiest and traverses a stony volcanic plateau, with mountains in the distance. There is a detour to Hafragilsfoss, another splendid waterfall just downstream with a viewpoint inside the dramatic Jökulsárgljúfur canyon (see p32). ◈ Map F2

Visitors at Dettifoss, Jökulsárgljúfur

A Day in the Lake Mývatn Area

Morning

Start early, and you can just about pack all of **Lake Mývatn**'s attractions (see pp16–17) into one long summer day. Begin with the subterranean hot pools at **Grjótagjá**, then move south to tackle **Hverfjall**'s slippery black slopes, making a circuit of the rim for spectacular views of the whole Mývatn area. Back at ground level, **Dimmuborgir** presents an extraordinary maze of natural lava sculptures (look for rare gyrfalcons nesting on rocky towers here), with only a short drive to the lakeshore at **Höfði Nature Park**, where you will definitely encounter numerous species of waterfowl, including barrow's goldeneye, scaup and mergansers. Follow the road to the south side of the lake at **Skútustaðir**, home to a large group of grassy pseudocraters.

Afternoon

Depending on your progress, you can grab lunch at the Dimmuborgir or Skútustaðir cafés, or circuit the lake to Reykjahlíð's **Gamli Bærinn**. Head east to the fearsome **Námaskarð** mud pits, set in a wasteland full of steam and eye-watering smells. A good side road runs north from here, via the Leirbotn Power Station, to where Víti volcano overlooks **Leirhnjúkur**, a huge expanse of steaming lava laid down in the 1980s – a place for careful explo- ration. Round off the day with a good soak on the way home at the **Jarðböðin** nature baths.

Left **Goðafoss** Right **Turf-roofed old farmhouse at Laufás**

Best of the Rest

1 Hofsós
Hard winters combined with a volcanic eruption at Askja in 1875 *(see p39)*, ended the livelihoods of many farmers, who as a result emigrated to Canada.

2 Glaumbær
Classic turf farmhouses built between 1750–1879. The use of imported timber hints at the family's comparative wealth. ⊗ *Map D2 • Glaumbær, 556 Varmahlíð • 453 6173 • Open 1 Jun–10 Sep 9am–6pm daily • Adm • www.skagafjordur.is*

3 Goðafoss
This impressive waterfall is named after events that occured when Christianity was introduced here in AD 1000 *(see p33)*.

4 Vaglaskógur
This beautiful, extensive stretch of birch woodland along Fnjóskadalur Valley is a popular camping area with a small store and walking trails. ⊗ *Map E2 • Campsite open 1 Jun–31 Aug; 860 2213*

5 Laufás
The museum here, housed in a 19th-century turf farmhouse, displays period household objects. The adjacent church is a little older with a 17th-century pulpit. ⊗ *Map E2 • 463 3196 • Open 30 May–12 Sep 9am–6pm daily • Adm*

6 Grenjaðarstaður
Some of the buildings here have flowers on their turf roofs. Check out the headstones carved with runes in the cemetery. ⊗ *Map E2 • 464 3688 • Open Jun–Aug 10am–6pm daily • Adm*

7 Laxá í Aðaldal
Better known for its fishing potential further downstream, the Laxá's turbulent flow as it exits Lake Mývatn is a magnet for red-necked phalarope, barrow's goldeneye and harlequin duck *(see p64)*.

8 Þingeyrarkirkja
Built from solid stone blocks between 1909 and 1911, this remarkable church sits alone on a vegetated sandbar *(see p67)*. ⊗ *Map C2 • Þingeyrar, near Blönduós • Open Jun–Aug 10am–5pm daily*

9 Hvítserkur
The natural rock formation resembling a 15-m (49-ft) tall dinosaur drinking from the sea, lies on the east of the Vatnsnes Peninsula on Route 711. ⊗ *Map C4*

10 Tjörnes
This rounded peninsula with distinct banded geological strata yields bivalve and plant fossils. A signposted fossil bed is located near Ytri-Tunga farm. ⊗ *Map E2*

Price Categories

For a three course meal for one (without alcohol), with taxes and extra charges.

k	under ISK3,000
kk	ISK3,000–5,000
kkk	ISK5,000–7,000
kkkk	ISK7,000–9,000
kkkkk	over ISK9,000

Left **The restaurant at Hótel Gígur**

🔟 Places to Eat

Hótel KEA
1 Owned by the company that built Akureyri, this restaurant in Hótel KEA *(see p130)* offers every-thing from lunch buffets to á la carte dining. The wooden interior is dimly lit. ⌖ *kkkk*

Gamli Bærinn
2 The café-bar in Hótel Reynihlíð serves beer, light meals, snacks and coffee through the day. Gamli Bærinn's hearty traditional lamb soup is legendary. ⌖ *Map F2 • Reykjahlíð, Mývatn • 464 4170 • Open May–Aug 10am–midnight daily • kk*

Hótel Gígur
3 This hotel restaurant *(see p130)* has a beautiful setting with views out over the pseudocraters on Mývatn's southern shore. Ser-ves local fish and lamb. ⌖ *Map F3*

Staðarskáli
4 On the highway, halfway on the long drive between Reykjavík and Akureyri, pull up at this road-house to stretch your legs over coffee and a burger. ⌖ *Map C3 • Vegamót, Hrútafjörður • 451 1150 • k*

Bautinn/Smiðjan
5 Unpretentious restaurant that has been around for a long time and serves reliably tasty grilled beef, lamb and seafood main courses. ⌖ *Map E2 • Hafnarstræti 92, Akureyri • 462 1818 • kkk*

Bláa Kannan
6 Unmistakable corrugated iron exterior painted dark blue, with tables spilling on to the street, this is your best bet in town for coffee, cake and people watching. ⌖ *Map E2 • Hafnarstræti 96, Akureyri • 461 4600 • Open summer: 8:30am–11:30pm, winter: 9am–11pm • k*

Við Árbakkan
7 Blönduós has two places to eat and fortunately Við Árbakkan's tasty sandwiches, soups and grills save you from having to brave the petrol station's canteen. ⌖ *Map D2 • Húnabraut, Blönduós • 898 4678 • kkk*

Gamli Baukur
8 Set inside restored wooden warehouses overlooking the harbour, this snug place serves excellent soups, fish stews and burgers, all at a very reasonable cost given the size of the por-tions. ⌖ *Map F2 • Harbour, Húsavík • 464 2442 • Open 11:30am–midnight • kk*

Salka
9 Offering competition to the nearby Gamli Baukur, this restau-rant has a similar menu but with the bonus of outdoor tables when there is sunshine, at least. ⌖ *Map E2 • Garðarsbraut 6, Húsavík • 464 2551 • kk*

Greifinn
10 A no-nonsense pizza restaurant, with an extensive menu. It is also a nice place to sit and eat if you do not fancy takeaway. ⌖ *Map E2 • Glerágata 20, Akureyri • 460 1600 • Open 11:30am–10pm Mon–Thu, 11:30am–11pm Fri–Sat • k*

Left **Turf house at Bakkagerði** Right **Lagarfljót river near Egilsstaðir**

East Iceland

EAST ICELAND COVERS A VARIED REGION *of broad river valleys, boggy plateaus surrounding the mighty Vatnajökull icecap, and a dramatically compressed coastline forming the East Fjords. The main centres are Egilsstaðir on the shores of forested Lake Lögurinn and Höfn, a springboard for the main Vatnajökull National Park. Visiting smaller communities such as Vopnafjörður, Bakkagerði and Seyðisfjörður (with its international ferry) provides an insight into the daily life here, while rewarding side-trips include a visit to Papey Island or the remote Kárahnjúkar hydro dam.*

Puffins on Papey island

🔟 Sights

1. Egilsstaðir
2. Hallormsstaður
3. Skriðuklaustur
4. Vatnajökull National Park
5. Bakkagerði (Borgafjörður eystri)
6. Seyðisfjörður
7. Mjóifjörður
8. Vopnafjörður
9. Papey
10. Höfn

Egilsstaðir

Just east of the elongated Lake Lögurinn, Egilsstaðir lies at the junction with Route 1 and several smaller roads radiating coastwards to the scattered East Fjord communities. An unpretentious service centre with a variety of accommodation, restaurants and well-stocked shops. Attractions include the East Iceland Museum, featuring a Viking burial site and reconstructed traditional turf houses; and the 70 km (44-mile) drive around Lögurinn to take in saga sites, extensive woodlands and one of Iceland's tallest waterfalls. ◈ *Map G3* • *Summer-only buses from Akureyri and Reykjavík via Höfn. Airport open year-round* • *Museum: open Jun–Sep: 11am–5pm daily, adm*

Egilsstaðir town, near Lake Lögurinn

Hallormsstaður

Southwest of Egilsstaðir, lakeshore Hallormsstaður sits beside Iceland's most extensive forest, grown since the 1900s for recreational use and for timber. A web of wooded walking trails heads up the valley slopes, while a roadside Forestry Office has a small arboretum with 40 tree species as well as Iceland's tallest, a 22-m- (62-ft-) high larch. Near the lake is pretty Atlavík Bay with scented birch surrounding the camping ground. ◈ *Map G3*

Skriðuklaustur

This imposing stone-built villa belonging to author Gunnar Gunnarsson (1889–1975) sits on Lögurinn's western shore, close to the church at Valþjófstaður, Hengifoss, and the road to Kárahnjúkar. Gunnar's series of novels about Icelandic farm life, *Af Borgslægtens Historie*, were later filmed. Besides acting as a Visitor Centre for Vatnajökull National Park, there is a gallery here that hosts regular exhibitions. The attached Klausturkaffi offers a coffee buffet with excellent home-made cakes. ◈ *Map G3* • *471 2990* • *Open May–15 Sep: 10am–6pm daily* • *www.skriduklaustur.is*

Vatnajökull National Park

The bulk of Europe's largest national park surrounds the Vatnajökull icecap itself, whose eastern fringes are 100 km (62 miles) southwest of Egilsstaðir or 10 km (6 miles) northwest from Höfn. Direct access points include the Kárahnjúkur road west of Egilsstaðir, for which you will need a 4WD, or hiking tracks through Lónsöræfi Reserve *(see p102)*. Skidoo trips from Höfn will get you to the ice and the various glacier tongues can also be viewed from here *(see pp18–19)*. ◈ *Map F4*

A view of the Vatnajökull icecap

Héraðsflói's Birdlife

Héraðsflói – a broad bay with black-sand beach and boggy meadows inland along the myriad streamlets of the Jökulsá á Brú river – makes a superb place for observing birdlife. Look for marine ducks (including the long-tailed or old squaw and scoter), godwit, red-throated divers and even hobbys, Iceland's smallest bird of prey.

Church on Seyðisfjörður's main street

5 Bakkagerði (Borgafjörður eystri)

Part of the fun of visiting Bakkagerði, East Fjord's most endearing settlement, is the journey via the Héraðsflói estuary's grassy lagoons and steep ranges that isolate the village. On arrival you will find a tiny community backed by jagged Dyrfjöll mountain, with sights including a little hummock near the church named Álfaborg, home to Iceland's fairy queen, and a sizeable puffin colony overlooking the fishing harbour. Superb, lengthy hiking trails lead south to Seyðisfjörður. ✎ Map H2

6 Seyðisfjörður

Seyðisfjörður's charm lies in its steep fjord setting and 19th-century wooden architecture near the harbour. The church, several houses and two hotels are the pick, most painted in pastel hues and originally imported from Norway. An important naval station during World War II and a herring port before then, today Seyðisfjörður is linked to Norway by the *Nörunna* ferry, which visits weekly in summer via the Faroes and Denmark. ✎ Map H3

7 Mjóifjörður

A long, thin inlet accessed by the gravel Route 953, Mjóifjörður (Narrow Fjord) is worth the bumpy drive to Brekka village and the remote lighthouse at Dalatangi. The road between the shoreline and steep mountains offers some close-ups of beautiful streams and cascades, plus the chance of seeing the Arctic fox that are more at ease with humans in this remote area. ✎ Map H3

8 Vopnafjörður

If you are making the long coastal drive along Route 85 from Húsavík towards Egilsstaðir, set

Bakkagerði with the Dyrfjöll mountain in the background

aside an hour for Vopnafjörður, a small town built on a steep prong of land. It has a museum detailing the plight of local communities following the 1875 eruption of Víti at Askja *(see p39)*. An outdoor geothermal pool at Selárdalur and Bustarfell's immaculate collection of old turf farmhouses *(see p102)* are located close by. ◈ *Map G2*

Papey

The ferry ride to Papey is one of the highlights of East Iceland, taking in rock ledges full of snoozing seals, an ocean covered in seabirds flapping frantically out of the way of boats and the small, grass-topped island, thought to have been inhabited by monks before the Vikings arrived *(see p53)*. ◈ *Map H4*

Boats lined up at Höfn

Höfn

Höfn started as a warehouse during the 1860s, and has since developed into a small working port. The town makes a good base for trips to Vatnajökull National Park: the Glacier Exhibition fills you in on the area; you can book skiddoo trips and super-jeep tours to the icecap; while hikers can aim for Lónsöræfi Reserve. For glacier views, head for the landmark statue on the shore – avoiding the nearby Arctic tern colony. ◈ *Map G5 • Year-round buses to Reykjavík, and summer services to Egilsstaðir, airport open year-round*

A Day in East Iceland

Morning

Before starting on this 70-km (44-mile) circuit of **Lake Lögurinn** and the Lagarfljót Valley, climb the hillock behind the Menntaskólinn school in **Egilsstaðir** for a view of the region – on a clear day you can see southwest over the lake as far as **Snæfell** *(see p102)*, Iceland's highest free-standing peak. Then head south, branching off the highway onto Route 931 past fields full of lambs and Icelandic horses, until a surprising amount of woodland begins to spring up around **Hallormsstaður**, where you can explore walking tracks or the Forestry Office's arboretum, or take in lakeside views at **Atlavík**. Exiting the woods past Atlavík, the main road crosses the lake to Lögurinn's west shore, where you turn left and drive some distance to **Skriðuklaustur**.

Afternoon

After having a snack at Skriðuklaustur's café, **Klausturkaffi** and a look at the National Park exhibition, continue south to **Valþófsstaður** church with its reproduction of carved Viking doors, then retrace your route back past Skriðuklaustur to where the 60-km- (37-mile-) long Route 910 ascends to moorlands around Snæfell and the **Kárahnjúkar hydro dam** *(see p102)*. You need three hours for this round trip, otherwise follow an hour-long walking track uphill to **Hengifoss** *(see p102)* after parking your car. Stay on the western shore for the drive back to Egilsstaðir.

Left **Hengifoss, dropping into a gorge** Right **Flock of geese in a field, Eyjabakkar**

Best of the Rest

Hengifoss
This 118-m (387-ft) fall is Iceland's third-highest, dropping in a narrow ribbon off a cliff-face layered in red and black. On the way up don't miss the twisted basalt columns at Litlifoss. ◈ *Map G3*

Steinasafn Petru
Extensive private geological collection, featuring coloured stones, crystals and mineral samples from all over the world. Owner does not speak English. ◈ *Map H4 • Sunnuhlíð, Stöðvarfjörður, East Fjords • 475 8843, 475 8839 • Open May–Sep: 9am–6pm daily • Adm*

Hvítserkur
Spectacular, orange, pink and grey rhyolite mountain 10 km (6 miles) along a hiking trail from Bakkagerði – the colours really stand out after rain. The trail is straightforward, but be prepared for changing weather. ◈ *Map H3*

Snæfell
This isolated, snow-capped granite core of an old volcano lies at Vatnajökull's northeast corner. It is located on a 4WD-only track. Hiking huts around the base. ◈ *Map F4 • www.vatnajokulsthjodgardur.is*

Kárahnjúkar Hydro Dam
Controversial project that dammed the Dimmugljúfur canyon to provide power for a smelter. The sealed road crosses highland tundra, full of reindeer. ◈ *Map F4*

Lónsöræfi
Wild, uninhabited area, rich in gorges, moorland and glacier scenery. An unmarked, 5-day trail for self-sufficient hikers runs from Stafafell to Snæfell. ◈ *Map G4 • www.vatnajokulsthjodgardur.is*

Eyjabakkar
Boggy highland region en route to Kárahnjúkar or Snæfell, it is a breeding ground for greylag geese and whooper swans; reindeer are common too.

Valþjófstaður
Farm and red-roofed church, with replica carved Viking panels as doors. The originals are in Reykjavík's National Museum. ◈ *Map G3 • Open 10am–5pm daily*

Lagarfljótsormur
A riverboat, named after a legendary serpent said to inhabit Lögurinn, which cruises down the lake to Atlavík. ◈ *847 2524*

Bustarfell
Well-preserved turf-roofed farmhouses (rebuilt in 1770), occupied by the same family since 1532. Café on site. ◈ *Map G2 • 473 1466 • Open 10 Jun–10 Sep: 10am–6pm daily • Adm*

Left **Café Nielsen, Egilsstaðir**

Places to Eat

1 Fjallakaffi
This café is attached to the highest farm in Iceland and can be reached along Route 901 south off Route 1 from Lake Mývatn. Accommodation is also available here. Ⓢ *Map F3 • Mörðrudal á Fjöllum • 471 1858, 894 8181 • k*

2 Hótel Hérað
Local reindeer steak is the obvious thing to try at Hérað's restaurant, although they also offer lamb and seafood dishes *(see p130).* Ⓢ *kkkk*

3 Café Nielsen
Located in an old wooden building, this restaurant-bar has an outdoor deck downstairs. Try the lunch buffets, soup and salad to keep the costs down. Grilled fish and lamb are excellent. Ⓢ *Map G3 • Tjarnarbraut 1, Egilsstaðir • 471 2626 • Open summer: 11:30am–11:30pm & 1pm–2am Fri–Sat, winter: 11:30am–10pm Mon–Thu 1pm–1am Fri–Sat • kkk*

4 Hótel Hallormstaður
Popular fixed-price lunch and dinner buffets with cold smoked lamb, bread, soup and all the usual suspects. It is a café for the rest of the day. Nice setting and friendly service *(see p132).* Ⓢ *k*

5 Klausturkaffi
Home-made wild mushroom soup is a speciality, along with reindeer and goose dishes (menu changes regularly). Also renowned for its coffee and cakes. Ⓢ *Map G3 • Skriðuklaustur • 471 2992 • kkk*

6 Hótel Tangi
The hotel restaurant is the most popular place to eat in town. Their pizzas, burgers and grilled fish are done well. Ⓢ *Map G2 • Hafnarbyggð 17, Vopnafjörður • 473 1840 • kkk*

7 Hótel Aldan
Beautiful wooden dining room in a pretty wood building, this is a great place to eat an early cooked breakfast or an elegant three-course dinner. Their fish dishes are outstanding *(see p132).* Ⓢ *kkk*

8 Hótel Framtíð
Good place at Djúpivogur's harbour to fill up on hearty pasty, fish and lamb dishes before making the trip over to Papey island *(see p130).* Ⓢ *kkk*

9 Álfacafé
Housed inside a former fish factory near Bakkagerði's old harbour, with astonishingly heavy tables and crockery made out of solid stone. Only light meals served, but their sandwiches are good. Ⓢ *Map H2 • Bakkagerði • 892 4880, 472 9884 • Open summer: 11am–8pm daily • k*

10 Kaffi Hornið
Warm up inside this timber building on Höfn's main street, with soup, pasta, pizza and grills, along with coffee and the inevitable cakes, served on checkered tablecloths. Ⓢ *Map G5 • Hafnarbraut 42, Höfn • 478 2600 • kkk*

Left **Basalt cliffs near Vík** Right **Main bathing pool at the Blue Lagoon**

South Iceland

SOUTH ICELAND FORMS AN EXTRAORDINARILY RICH *and long band of coastline, minor icecaps, fertile river plains and explosive volcanic landscapes, all wrapped up in history and folklore. The Blue Lagoon and the "Golden Circle," which includes Þingvellir, Geysir and Gullfoss, are Iceland's most iconic tourist sights. There is also the Hekla volcano, a wealth of saga locations, some waterfalls, access to hiking grounds at Landmannalaugar and Þórsmörk, the gem-like but often-overlooked Westman Islands and peaceful Vík village, all within easy reach from Reykjavík. East of Vík, you will need more time to reach Kirkjubæjarklaustur town, the Jökulsárlón glacial lagoon and the fringes of Vatnajökull National Park at Skaftafell and Höfn.*

Sights

1. Þingvellir National Park
2. Geysir
3. Gullfoss
4. The Blue Lagoon
5. Þjórsárdalur
6. Vestmannaeyjar
7. Markarfljót Valley
8. Vík
9. Kirkjubæjarklaustur
10. Jökulsárlón

A view of the settlement at Vík

Preceding pages **Hiking in the Landmannalaugar area**

1 Þingvellir National Park

This amazing rift valley, now a UNESCO World Heritage site, was the setting for Iceland's open-air parliament in Viking times. Stop at the Visitor Centre on the way along Route 36 for superlative views over the rift walls and the lava plains. Spend a few minutes picking out key features such as the Law Rock, Þingvellir Church, Almannagjá canyon, Öxarárfoss, Þingvallavatn lake and the Skjaldbreiður volcano (see pp8–9).

Gullfoss seen from the middle viewpoint

2 Geysir

It is incredible to find such a raw, primal sight as Geysir's scalding water spouts erupting by the side of the main road. Just 90 minutes from the capital, Geysir has a hotel, petrol station and tourist centre alongside. The key geysir to watch here is Strokkur, but if you are lucky the original vent, Geysir itself, might blow its top. The whole site is surrounded by a collection of smaller hot pools, each with its own distinct character (see pp12–13).

3 Gullfoss

The final stop on a tour of the "Golden Circle", Gullfoss is Iceland's most dramatic waterfall and deafening, except in winter. Make sure you get a look from

Hot pools of Blesi, Geysir

as many viewpoints as possible, especially from the top of the canyon, from where you can appreciate the Hvítá river's journey from the barren Interior to the north (see pp14–15).

4 The Blue Lagoon

Iceland's southwest extreme, the Reykjanes Peninsula is almost entirely covered in barren lava fields, which makes finding the vivid Blue Lagoon hidden within it doubly surprising. Creative use of waste-water from a geothermal power plant and the outdoor soak at the Blue Lagoon makes for an outstanding experience. Its white silt is said to have health benefits too (see pp10–11).

5 Þjórsárdalur

Þjórsárdalur is a broad, stark river valley, sterilized by a huge eruption in 1102 of the Hekla volcano, just one ridge away to the east. The eruption buried a Viking longhouse up the valley at Stöng, now excavated and open to the public via a rough, gravel track, with a full reconstruction nearby at Þjóðveldisbærinn. Up a parallel track, Þjórsárdalslaug is a great open-air pool where you can lounge amidst the valley's harsh natural splendour. ◆ Map D5 • Stöng road subject to closure • Þjóðveldisbærinn: 1 Jun–31 Aug: 10am–noon & 1–6pm daily; Þjórsárdalslaug:1 Jun–31 Aug: 1–7pm Wed–Fri, noon–7pm Fri–Sat • Adm

Njál's Saga

A gripping account of a bloody, 50-year-long family feud revolving around the household of Njáll Þorgeirsson, in which the evil schemings of Mörð Valgarðsson causes the deaths of both Njáll and his friend Gunnar Hámundarson. The hard-boiled delivery is softened by deadpan humour and vivid insights into daily life during Viking times.

Hikers on a trail, Skaftafell National Park

Vestmannaeyjar

6 The Westman Islands are a string of volcanic outcrops off the south coast which include the world's newest island, Surtsey *(see p53)*. Heimaey is the largest and only inhabited island in the group, famous for the 1973 Eldfell eruption, which partially buried Heimaey town, almost ending its fishing industry. Stay overnight and climb Eldfell's still-steaming slopes, walk around the coast in half a day, visit the wooden Nordic church, look out for puffins or enjoy the Þjóðhátíð festival *(see p55)*. ✎ *Map C6 • Daily ferry from Þorlakshöfn, flights from Reykjavík & Bakki.*

Markarfljót Valley

7 To reach the pretty valley of Markarfljót, take Route 1 to Hvolsvöllur township – where you should visit the excellent

Saga Centre – and then follow the 30-km- (19-mile-) long Route 261 east. The area is central to key scenes from *Njál's Saga*, including the farm Völlur, where the tale opens; and Hlíðarendi, home to the virtuous Gunnar Hámundarson. There is a church on the hillside at Hlíðarendi today, from where you can look seawards over the valley, where landmarks like rocky Stóri-Dímon stand proud. ✎ *Map D5 • Saga Centre: open Jun–15 Sep 9am–6pm daily, adm, www.njala.is*

Vík

8 This peaceful seafront community of around 300 people is located below Reynisfjall's tall cliffs, with a dramatic black-sand beach, great views west over the flat Mýrdalssandur, lively bird colonies and some towering offshore black stacks known as the Troll Rocks. Skógar and its waterfall are just up the road *(see p33)*. There are more sea-scapes west around the corner at Reynisfjall and Dyrhólaey *(see p34)*. Also close by are a number of walking tracks. All in all, this is a great place to chill out for a few days. ✎ *Map D6*

Black beach, west of Dyrhólaey

9 Kirkjubæjarklaustur

A tiny highway town in the middle of nowhere, Kirkjubæjarklaustur is surrounded by pseudocraters and hexagonal lava pavements known as Kirkjugólf (church floor), with summer access to the awesome Lakagígar craters *(see pp38–9)*. The town's name – literally Church Farm Monastery – reflects its origins in 1186 as a convent. Moving west, Skaftafell in Vatnajökull National Park *(see pp18–19)* is not too far on the other side of the black, sandy spread of the Skeiðarársandur desert. Map E5

10 Jökulsárlón

An essential stop on the long journey between Vík and Höfn, Jökulsárlón's icebergs, glacier tongue and rushing waters – not to mention the bizarre sight of ice boulders on the beach – break the monotony of bleak expanses of black gravel along the coastal fringes. Seals and occasional orca (killer whales) are the pick of wildlife commonly encountered here, although there is plenty of birdlife too. Half-hour lagoon cruises are an option in summer *(see pp26–7)*. Map G5

Icebergs at Jökulsárlón

A Day in South Iceland

Morning

Begin a classic "Golden Circle" tour by heading northeast from Reykjavík up Route 36, looking out along the way for the boxy, two-storey white house of the late author and Nobel Laureate Halldór Laxness. After reaching Þingvallavatn's blue spread you arrive on the west side of the **Þingvellir** rift valley, where it is time to spend an hour – or the entire day – soaking up the events and landscapes at Iceland's cultural heart. Cross the rift and take Route 365 to **Laugarvatn**, where you could stop and have a swim at the National School for Sports, before pressing further along routes 37 and 35 to spectacular water features at **Geysir** and **Gullfoss**.

Afternoon

Have lunch at either Hótel Geysir – where you can get a proper three-course meal – or at Gullfoss' Visitor Centre, whose café does excellent lamb soup. Then follow Route 35 southwest to **Skálholt** *(see p66)* a bishopric and educational centre since the 11th century. Route 35 continues southwest from Skálholt past the **Kerið** crater *(see p110)* to **Selfoss**, a busy town on the River Ölfusá, whose bridge was the cause of Iceland's first strike. The highway runs straight back to Reykjavík via the hothouse town of **Hveragerði** (famous for its flowers and vegetables), or you can detour coastwards to the villages of **Stokkseyri** and **Eyrarbakki** *(see p110)*.

Left **Skógar Museum** Right **Bridge between two continents, near Keflavík**

🔟 Best of the Rest

1 Mýrdalsjökull
This impressive south-coast icecap conceals the dangerous Katla volcano. The lowest glacier tongue, Solheimsjökull, is accessible off Route 1, where you can ice-climb, ride a snow-mobile or go dogsledding. ⬡ *Map D6* • *www. mountainguides.is; www.snow.is; www. dogsledding.is*

2 Kerið Crater
Beautiful, deep but small crater, north of Selfoss, best viewed on a sunny day to appreciate the red and black slopes contrasting with the blue water.

3 Skógar
Tiny community at the foot of Skógafoss *(see p33)*, with a hotel, hostel and campsite but little else apart from the Skógar Museum *(see p62)* and a superb hike to Þórsmörk *(see p57)*.

4 Hveragerði
Iceland's major hothouse town, using geothermal heat to grow flowers and vegetables on commercial scale. There is a horticultural college, hiking trails and a swimming pool. ⬡ *Map C5*

5 Leirubakki
Farm and hotel on mount Hekla, with a volcano museum and lava-block hot tub with views of the mountain, on the road to Landmannalaugar *(see pp24–5)*.
⬡ *Map D5* • *Route 26* • *487 8700*
• *Summer buses between Reykjavík and Landmannalaugar* • *www.leirubakki.is*

6 Hafnir Continental Bridge
The European and American continental plates separate most visibly at Þingvellir – the bridge allows you to cross between the continents. ⬡ *Map C5*

7 Sandgerði Nature Centre
Very unusual museum full of microscopic sea creatures. Do not miss the stuffed walrus. ⬡ *Map B5*
• *Fræðasetrið, Garðvegur 1, Sandgerði*
• *423 7551* • *Open 9am–5pm Mon–Fri, 1–5pm Sat & Sun* • *Adm* • *www.sandgerdi.is*

8 Hvolsvöllur Saga Centre
Lively exhibition of Viking era mannequins, models and maps.
⬡ *Map C6* • *Hlíðarvegur 14, Hvolsvöllur*
• *487 8781* • *Open summer: 9am–6pm Jun–15 Sep* • *Adm* • *www.njala.is*

9 Þórbergssetur
Museum dedicated to writer Þórbergur Þórðarson (1888–1974), is located in his home, also now a hotel. ⬡ *Map G5* • *Hali,781 Hornarfjörður*
• *478 1078* • *Adm* • *www.thorbergssetur.is*

10 Stokkseyri and Eyrarbakki
Two delightful villages with a maritime heritage, old wooden houses, great seafood restaurants and the Húsið museum. ⬡ *Map C5*
• *Húsið museum: www.husid.com*

Above **Exterior of Hótel Rangá, near Selfoss**

Price Categories

For a three course meal for one (without alcohol), with taxes and extra charges.

k	under ISK3,000
kk	ISK3,000–5,000
kkk	ISK5,000–7,000
kkkk	ISK7,000–9,000
kkkkk	over ISK9,000

🔟 Places to Eat

1 Hótel Rangá
Nordic-European cuisine is served at this splendid restaurant in a rural hotel *(see p130)* with views of the finest salmon river in the country. Make sure you try the venison with wild mushrooms and berries. 🟣 kkkk

2 Menam
A great Thai place outside Reykjavík with all the favourites, from green curry to spicy prawn soup cooked absolutely fresh. No MSG used. 🟣 *Map C5 • Eyravegur 8, Selfoss • 482 4099 • kkk*

3 Hótel Geysir
Generous breakfast and lunch buffets and great views of the geysir area, make this hotel restaurant the best place to eat in the area. 🟣 *Map C5 • Haukadalur, Geysir • 480 6800 • kkk*

4 Hótel Selfoss
Styled with a minimalist Nordic look, this upmarket option is more comfortable than it appears, with a well-presented menu of Icelandic seafood and meat staples. Good place to impress a client. 🟣 *Map C5 • Eyravegur 2, Selfoss • 480 2500 • kkkk*

5 Gullfoss Kaffi
With wide vistas of the surrounding landscape – though not of Gullfoss itself – this spacious, wooden-framed café is a great spot to pull up for a bowl of lamb soup. 🟣 *Map D4 • Gullfoss • 486 6500 • k*

6 Hótel Flúðir
Oddly aloof modern building on the edge of a farming town, Flúðir has splendid views and a menu featuring locally-grown hothouse vegetables and native meats. 🟣 *Map C5 • Vesturbrún 1, Flúðir • 486 6630 • kkk*

7 Rauða Húsið
A good reason to visit the charming Eyrarbakki village, this restaurant set in an old wooden house offers splendid lobster, lamb and fish dishes at a fraction of their cost in Reykjavík. 🟣 *Map C5 • Búðarstíg 4, Eyrarbakki • 483 3330 • kkk*

8 Hafið Bláa
Another good choice at the mouth of the Ölfusá river, where you should forget the other choices and just focus on their exceptional grilled lobster. 🟣 *Map C5 • Þorlákshöfn, near Óseyrar Bridge, Eyrarbakki • 483 1000 • kkkk*

9 Kaffi Duus
Smart place not far from the Keflavík International Airport, so a good choice to tuck into lamb, lobster or salmon before heading homewards. 🟣 *Map B5 • Duusgata 10, Keflavík • 421 7080 • kkkk*

10 Hlíðarendi
A no-nonsense café inside Hvolsvöllur's main petrol station, but a handy pit-stop for tasty burgers, pizza and coffee after hiking in Þórsmörk. 🟣 *Map C6 • Austurvegur 3, Hvolsvöllur • 487 8197 • k*

Left **Hot pool at Hveravellir** Right **Campsite at Landmannalaugar**

The Highland Interior

INLAND FROM THE RELATIVELY FERTILE COASTLINE, *Iceland's Highland Interior is a beautiful wilderness of black gravel, lava plains and glaciated peaks, blasted by summer storms and severe winter frosts. Not surprisingly, the Interior has never been settled, but it remained crossed by the ghosts of numerous pack-horse trails used from Viking times until Route 1 around the country was completed in the 1970s. Open for just a few weeks in summer to 4WDs only, the most accessible of these routes are the Kjölur (from Gullfoss to near Akureyri) and Fjallabak (from Hella to Kirkjubæjarklaustur). Long-distance buses also follow these routes from June to September.*

🔟 Sights

1. The Kjölur Route
2. Hveravellir
3. Mount Hekla
4. Landmannalaugar
5. Veiðivötn & Langisjór
6. Þórsmörk Reserve
7. Lakagígar
8. Langjökull
9. Aldeyjarfoss
10. Herðubreið

View of the Langajökull glacier, from the Kjölur highway

1 The Kjölur Route
The Kjölur Route (Kjalvegur) is the least difficult of the Highland roads, running for 170 km (106 miles) from Gullfoss *(see pp14–15)* to Route 1 near Blönduós *(see p93)*. All the major rivers have been bridged and the well-formed gravel track is safe. Sights along the way include Hveravellir's hot springs and the Langjökull icecap.
⊛ *Map D4 • Bus schedule: www.bsi.is • Road open mid-Jun–late Aug*

2 Hveravellir
Halfway along the Kjölur Route, Hveravellir is a desolate hot-springs area with an outdoor hot-tub, calcified mounds bubbling out boiling water, a strong smell of sulphur, and a basic hut with bunkbeds run by the Icelandic Touring Club (www.fi.is). The 17th-century outlaw Eyvindur spent many winters here till local farmers chased him out. ⊛ *Map D4*

3 Mount Hekla
East of Þjórsá river is Mount Hekla, which means "hooded," after the clouds that obscure its summit. It was once believed to be the entrance to hell, due to its eruptions followed by months of

Hikers on the Laugavegur trail

Þjórsá river, west of Mount Hekla

noisy "grumbling" (taken to be the sound of tormented souls). On a good day, you can see the mountain from Hella on Route 1, and you will pass close to it en route Landmannalaugar. Many companies run super-jeep circuits and trips to the mountain during summer. ⊛ *Map D5*

4 Landmannalaugar
Relatively accessible and just 3 or 4 hours from Reykjavík, Landmannalaugar delivers a full Highland experience. The road traverses volcanic wastelands, exciting river crossings, mountains and hot springs. There are enough hills, lava fields and lakes to explore for a day. You could even stay at the bunkhouse or the camp and spend 4 days hiking to Þórsmörk along the Laugavegur trail *(see p25)*. ⊛ *Map D5*

5 Veiðivötn and Langisjór
Veiðivötn and Langisjór are part of a complex of inland waterways inside volcanic "stretch marks" southwest from Vatnajökull, reached off the F208 Fjallabak Route. There are some good fishing areas and unbelievably stark country. Veiðivötn is an area of tarns and streams while Langisjór is a narrow stretch of water. Both are accessible only along rough tracks and there is no public transport. ⊛ *Map E5*

A cliff above Gullfoss

6 Þórsmörk Reserve

Iceland's most popular hiking area, accessible only in a 4WD from the highway near Hvolsvöllur via the 30-km- (19-mile-) long F249 – though watch out for the potentially dangerous river crossing at the end – or by trekking in along Laugavegur or from Skógar via Fimmvörðuháls (see p56). Set in an exceptionally pretty glacial valley, pick of the views at Þórsmörk are from Valahnúkur, an easy and short ascent and the arduous and long Utigönguhöfði. There are plenty of self-catering cabins and campsites, and daily buses through the summer (see p57). ◈ Map D6

7 Lakagígar

This 25-km- (16-mile-) long row of craters erupted with a vengeance in 1783, disrupting weather patterns all across Europe and nearly depopulating Iceland. Walking trails ranging between 20 minutes and 2 hours allow you to explore the line of cones and expansive lavafields, now partly buried under a thick matting of moss and heather. There is no accommodation on site, but mountain huts and campsites can be found along the road. Seasonal buses from Skaftafell National Park run here via Kirkjubæjarklaustur and the 60-km- (37-mile-) long F206 (see p19). ◈ Map E5 • Buses: 1 Jul–31 Aug daily; schedule: www.re.is

8 Langjökull

Iceland's second largest icecap, the "Long Glacier" west of the Kjölur Route feeds Hvítárvatn and Sandvatn lakes, which in turn drain into the Hvítá river on which the spectacular Gullfoss waterfalls are located (see pp14–15). There is talk of damming another of its lakes, Hagavatn, for hydro power. Apart from seeing the glacier from the Kjölur or Kaldidalur routes, tours run up here for snowmobiling trips – you only get an hour but it is an exhilarating experience, like riding a jetski on snow. ◈ Map D4 • Year-round jeep tours from Reykjavík • www.explore.is

9 Aldeyjarfoss

Although these impressive falls on the Skjálfandafljót river sit

Eyjafjallajökull icecap from the summit of Valahnúkur

at the northern end of the otherwise difficult Sprengisandur Route, they are actually located on a good gravel road 30 km (19 miles) south of the Goðafoss waterfall *(see p33)*. Most vehicles can make it with care during the summer, but check conditions first. What makes Aldeyjarfoss so striking are the surrounding rock formations, where a layer of outlandishly fashioned basalt columns is capped by a thick blanket of solidified lava. Buses negotiating the Sprengisandur crossing between Reykjavík and Akureyri make it a point to stop here.
◈ *Map E3 • Bus schedule: www.re.is*

Basalt columns at Aldeyjarfoss

Herðubreið
Known as the "Queen of the Mountains", Herðurbreið's spiky palagonite heights rise to an impressive 1,682 m (5,518 ft) northeast of Askja above the dismal Ódáðahraun ("Desert of Evil Deeds"). The slopes are laced by short freshwater springs, covered with pink blooms of arctic river beauty in July. You get good views on a clear day from the road to Kárahnjúkar *(p102)*, but if you fancy hiking, stop on the F88 between Mývatn and Askja *(see pp16–17)*. ◈ *Map F3*

A Drive Through the Highlands

Morning

Start early for this day trip to **Landmannalaugar** and bring a packed lunch. This will take upwards of 8 hours, depending on how many times you stop along the way. Head east along Route 1 from Reykjavík via Selfoss and Hella, then turn north up Route 264 to Viking buildings at **Keldur** farm *(see pp62–3)*. With **Hekla** looming behind, take a moment to appreciate Keldur's location – so close to an active volcano. Retrace the route towards Hella, then turn north along Route 268 for a half-hour run through lava fields to Hekla and the inter-section with Route 26. You could turn left here to **Leirubakki** farm *(see p110)*, but for Landmannalaugar turn right, driving through the yellow pumice plain between Hekla and the þjórsá river, before reaching the F225 junction, which heads east to Landmannalaugar. Pull up and have lunch.

Afternoon

The F225 traverses the black sand wasteland of Hekla's northern foothills with several rivers before it reaches an intersection after 47 km (29 miles); turn right (south) down **Frostastaðavatn**'s lake-shore and then right again on to the 5-km- (3-mile-) long F224, which crosses a double fjord before reaching Landmannalaugar. Soak in the spring and then prepare to head back; once on Route 26 simply follow it south to the **Vegamót** road-house be-tween Hella and Selfoss.

STREETSMART

ICELAND'S TOP 10

Left **Tourist hut at Landmannalaugar** Right **Visitors on a puffin-viewing trip**

🔟 Planning Your Trip

1 Passports and Visas

Most visitors, including those from the UK and Ireland, Canada, the EU, USA, Australia, New Zealand and countries signed up to the Schengen Agreement, do not need a visa to enter Iceland for a visit under 90 days. You must have three months validity on your passport to enter the country. ◎ www.utl.is

2 Tourist Information

The main tourist information centre is in Reykjavík, offering information and brochures on accommodation, tours, dining, nightlife, money-saving cards and tax refunds. There are smaller offices at Keflavík airport and other towns.

3 Weather

Iceland's climate is temperate and milder than most people think. Temperature in summer can reach 23°C (74°F); winters are around 0°C (32°F). Autumn and spring are the wettest months. Snow is more common in the north than the south, which is warm and wet. ◎ www.vedur.is

4 When to Go

The midnight sun and summer temperatures make mid-June to mid-August the most popular time to visit. In the winter, lack of sunlight makes it less hospitable, and the

interior is not accessible (many bus routes to this part do not begin until late June when the snow melts). You stand a good chance of seeing the aurora borealis from November to February. Spring and autumn have roughly balanced periods of day and night.

5 What to Pack

Bring a variety of warm, wind and water-proof clothes as the weather can be unpredictable. Sunscreen, sunglasses and a good quality eye mask are vital during the summer. Hikers need sturdy hiking boots. Don't forget your camera and your swimming gear for the hot springs.

6 Time Zone

Iceland follows the Greenwich Mean Time and is 5 hours ahead of US Eastern Standard Time. It does not observe Daylight Saving Time.

7 Currency

The island's currency is the Icelandic króna (ISK) or krónur in plural. Money can be exchanged on arrival. Foreign currency is accepted at Keflavík airport and some shops in Reykjavík. MasterCard and Visa are accepted but in rural areas, cash is useful.

8 Insurance

This is relatively a safe country but you are advised to take out travel and health insurance and

check policy exclusions, especially if planning on hiking or adventure travel. Visitors from UK can take an EHIC health card, which covers basic national healthcare.

9 Current and Phone Adapters

Iceland has standard European electrical voltage and frequency (240V, 50Hz) so North American electrical devices will need converters. Plugs are two-pin and UK and North American items will need adapters. Most European mobile phones work on Iceland's GSM network but North American ones do not.

10 Special Equipment

Riding clothing and angling gear used outside Iceland must be disinfected, as per regulations and certified by a vet before entry. If not, it will be disinfected at your own cost. ◎ www.lbs.is

Directory

Tourist Information Offices
Map K2 • Aðalstræti 2, 101 Reykjavík • 590 1550 • www. visitreykjavik.is

Map B5 • Keflavík airport • 425 6010 • www.reykjanes.is

Map E2 • Hafnarstræti 82, Akureyri • 550 0720 • www.nordurland.is

Left **Sævar Karl, Reykjavík** Centre **Dómkirkjan, Reykjavík** Right **Thorvaldsen's bar, Reykjavík**

🔟 Useful Information

1 Useful Websites
The official tourist board website is www.visiticeland.com. Another good source of general information is www.icelandnaturally.com. The official Reykjavík website is www.visitreykjavik.is. Daily life and news on the island is covered on www.icelandreview.com. Foodies must visit www.icelandgourmetguide.com; hikers will like www.outdoors.is and www.nat.is while www.angling.is is for anglers. Weather information is at www.vedur.is. Younger visitors might like to visit www.grapevine.is to find out about nightlife; the selection of blogs on www.icelandexpress.com also provides a good flavour of the country.

2 Opening Hours
Office hours are Monday–Friday 9am–5pm, changing to 8am–4pm during June, July and August. Shops are open Monday–Friday 10am–6pm, Saturday from 10am until between 1 and 4pm. Some supermarkets are open until 11pm seven days a week. Banks are open Monday–Friday 9:15am–4pm. Outside Reykjavík, the hours may be shorter.

3 Public Holidays
Businesses, banks and most shops are closed on New Year's Day, Maundy Thursday, Good Friday, Easter Sunday, Easter Monday, First Day of Summer (usually third Thursday in Apr), Labour Day (May 1), Ascension Day, Whit Sunday, Whit Monday, National Day (Jun 17), Bank Holiday (First Monday in Aug), Christmas Eve (from noon), Christmas, Dec 26 and New Year's Eve (from noon).

4 Smoking Regulations
Since 2007, smoking has been prohibited in bars, restaurants, clubs and cafés across Iceland. There are no designated smoking areas inside and smoking outside is also restricted to some areas. You cannot smoke on public transport.

5 Embassies and Consulates
The foreign embassies in central Reykjavík include: USA: Laufásvegur 21, 562 9100, www.usa.is; UK: Laufásvegur 31, 550 5100, http://ukiniceland.fco.gov.uk/en; Canada: Túngata 14, 575 6500, www.canada.is; France: Túngata 22, 575 9600, www.ambafrance.is; Germany: Laufásvegur 31, 530 1100, www.reykjavik.diplo.de; Japan: Laugavegur 182, 6th floor, 510 8600, japan@itn.is.

6 Tipping
There is no tipping in Iceland – service charge is included in all bills. It may even be considered an insult to tip. You might make an exception for fishing guides but otherwise it is standard to pay the bill and no more.

7 Sale Periods
There are no regular sale periods in Iceland – they are at the retailer's discretion. Midsummer and January tend to see shops reducing prices.

8 Tax and VAT Refunds
All prices include VAT at 19.68%. Tourists get a 15% tax-free refund on single items costing ISK 4,000 or more. Ask for a tax-free form when buying. There are refund booths at Keflavík airport, on Seyðisfjörður ferries, at Reykjavík tourist office, and in Reykjavík malls.
🌐 www.icelandrefund.com

9 Electricity and Weights and Measures
Electricity is standard European 240V, 50 Hz. Weights and measures are metric.

10 Language
Icelanders learn English from an early age and most speak it well, albeit with a charming and quirky accent. You are only likely to find a language barrier if you were to speak in Icelandic since Icelanders are not used to foreigners trying to speak their language and usually just reply in English.

Left **Leifur Eiriksson Terminal, Keflavík International Airport** Right **Cruise liner, Reykjavik harbour**

🔟 Getting to Iceland

1 By Air
It takes about 3 hours to reach Iceland by air from Europe and 5–6 hours from the USA. Icelandair flies into Keflavík airport, 50 km (31 miles) from Reykjavík, from the USA, Canada and Europe. Budget airline Iceland Express flies into Keflavík from the US, UK and Europe and to Akureyri from Gatwick and Copenhagen.

2 Transport Security Regulations
Passengers can bring only a restricted quantity of liquids through security screening and in hand baggage. Each item may not exceed 100 ml (3.4 fl oz) of liquid and all containers must be carried in a 1-litre (34-fl oz) transparent plastic bag with a zip seal. Clearly labeled medication, baby food and foods for special diets may also be carried.

3 Duty Free Shopping
There is a duty free shop in the arrivals hall at Keflavík airport as well as in the departure lounge. Alcohol is significantly less expensive here than in the state-controlled alcohol shops in Iceland.

4 Leifur Eiríksson Terminal, Keflavík International Airport
The shops at Leifur Eiríksson Terminal offer a selection of international brands and exclusive local products, such as Blue Lagoon beauty treatments and Brennivín. There are also a number of bars and cafés. ◈ *Map B5 • 235 Keflavikurflugvollur • 425 6000 • www.kefairport.is*

5 Reykjavík Domestic Air Terminal
This small airport in central Reykjavík serves Greenland, the Faroe Islands and the rest of Iceland. Air Iceland flies from here to Akureyri, the Westman Islands, Egilsstaðir, Vopnafjörður, Grímsey and Ísafjörður. Eagle Air flies from here to Höfn, Sáuðárkrókur, Gjögur and Bíldudalur. Both run day tours of Iceland and Greenland. ◈ *Map L6 • Reykjavik airport, 101 Reykjavík • 424 4000 • www.flugstodir.is*

6 Other Domestic Air Terminals
Iceland's other airports *(see above)* are very small and serve only domestic flights with the exception of Akureyri which has flights to Copenhagen in the summer with Iceland Express and Egilsstaðir. They are mainly single runway airports with routes operated by Eagle Air or Air Iceland with multiple daily flights to Reykjavík.

7 Cheap Flights
Icelandair and Iceland Express regularly run sales on their websites. Sign up for email alerts from Iceland Express for the very cheapest deals on offer. Skyscanner is a good way to compare prices for the cheapest deals. The cheapest way to reach Reykjavík from Keflavík airport is on the Flybus. ◈ *www.icelandair. com; www.icelandexpress. com; www.skyscanner.net; www.flybus.is*

8 By Ferry
Smyril Line ferries sail from Denmark and the Faroe Islands to Seyðisfjörður weekly from April to October. It takes three nights from Denmark. You can take a car, campervan or motor-bike. It is not a budget option. ◈ *Yviri via Strond 1, Torshavn, Faroe Islands • 298 345900 • www. smyril-line.com*

9 By Cruise Ship
Plenty of cruise ships visit Iceland in summer, stopping at Reykjavík, Isafjörður, Akureyri and Seyðisfjörður. These include Princess Cruises, Holland America, P&O cruises, Hurtigruten, Fred Olsen Cruises, Cunard and Silversea. The itineraries include Spitsbergen, Greenland, Canada, north Europe and Arctic Circle.

10 Customs Allowances
Passengers above 18 can bring in 200 cigarettes or 250g of tobacco products and those above 20 may also bring one litre of spirits, a litre of wine or six litres of beer.

Left **A view from Perlan** Centre **Road sign** Right **Aircraft taking off from Ísafjörður Airport**

Getting Around Iceland

1 By Car
Driving is an easy way to get around Iceland (see p122). Be aware, however, that the roads are not perfect, especially outside metropolitan areas where they may not be sealed. Route 1 is the only motorway; it runs around the whole country for 1,300 km (808 miles). Some highland roads are closed in bad weather. ⊗ *www.vegagerdin.is/english*

2 Hiring a Car
There are car hire offices in Keflavík airport, downtown Reykjavík, Seyðisfjörður, Akureyri airport and other major towns around Iceland. You need a full international driving license and drivers under 25 may require additional cover. A 4WD is advised for driving in the interior and during the rains or winter.

3 By Bus
There are numerous daily services around Iceland from the BSÍ bus station in central Reykjavík. It takes seven hours to reach Akureyri. As there is no train service in Iceland, buses are the only means of public transport around the country besides domestic flights. Most services run daily or twice a day on weekends. ⊗ *Map L4 • Vatnsmýrarvegi 10, 101 Reykjavík • 562 1011 • 4:30am–midnight daily • www.bsi.is*

4 Taxis
Taxis in Iceland are metred and have uniform fares. There is no tipping. Look for ranks outside major hotels or call one. Many also offer sight-seeing tours and taxis to the airport ply at a fixed rate: ISK 11,000 for 1–4 passengers, ISK 13,000 for 5–8 passengers

5 Ferry
Ferries run to a number of important islands off the coast of Iceland. There are two daily services to the Westman Islands in the south, taking two hours 40 minutes. In the north, to reach Grímsey or Hrísey, you can take a daily ferry, and there are various ferry tours around the Western Fjords.

6 Cycling
Icelanders might laugh at you, but cycling has become an increasingly popular pursuit, despite unsealed gravel roads and unkind weather. There are several bike hire shops in Reykjavík and Akureyri. You are only permitted to cycle on roads, not off road as it might damage vulnerable vegetation.

7 Walking and Hiking
Reykjavík is small enough to walk around easily in a day, especially if you are staying in the 101 area. Hiking is popular around the country, particularly on the Landmannalaugar trail through the centre of Iceland. Websites on hiking trails are www.nat.is and www.outdoor.is.

8 Maps
You can purchase maps of Iceland in all good map and travel shops; in Reykjavík the bookshops Eymundsson and Mál og menning sell detailed hiking maps. Maps are also available via Icelandic online shops www.randburg.is and www.nordicstore.net. The tourist office can also provide maps. ⊗ *www.visiticeland.com*

9 GPS
GPS is the preferred method of navigation in Iceland as much of the country is uninhabited. With extreme weather conditions and a lack of mobile phone coverage, the highlands and a few rural areas can be dangerous without it. Some car rentals also offer GPS rental for the duration of your trip.

10 Seasonal Considerations
Transport here is subject to seasonal variation. Summer bus routes (June–August) are more frequent and winter services can be much reduced. Many mountain roads open only from July to mid-September. Domestic flights often get cancelled in bad weather and ferries take longer if the sea is rough. ⊗ *www.vedur.is*

Left **Gravel road** Centre **Petrol station, Ísafjörður** Right **Counters at domestic airport, Reykjavík**

🔟 Driving Tips

1 Driver's License and Insurance
All European and US driving licenses are valid in Iceland; UK visitors require both parts of their license. Visitors from other countries should check with their local motoring organizations. European drivers who bring their own vehicles do not need a Green Card or proof of third party insurance.

2 Car Rental Agencies
Downtown Reykjavík, Keflavík airport and Akureyri have many international and local car rental agencies; Iceland Express and Icelandair offer flydrive packages including car hire. The minimum age for hiring a car is 21 and 25 for jeeps. Hire cars may not be insured for highland driving.

3 Fuel
Fuel is priced by the litre. Self-service pumps are cheaper than attended ones; Atlantsolia and ÓB are the cheapest brands. Fill up when you can in rural areas. Most filling stations are open till 11:30pm. Those in Reykjavík and large towns often have automatic payment after closing time, accepting Visa credit cards and notes.

4 Speed Limits and Laws
The speed limit is 50 kmph (30 mph) unless otherwise marked. It is 80 kmph (50 mph) on gravel roads, 90 kmph (56 mph) on asphalt and 30 kmph (19 mph) in residential areas. Drivers and passengers must wear seat belts and headlights must be on at all times. Driving is on the right. It is against the law to drive after drinking alcohol.

5 Parking
Some Icelanders do not parallel park and might leave vehicles at strange angles anywhere along the street. Laws advise parking in the direction of traffic, 16 ft (5 m) from pedestrian crossings and intersections. Parking restrictions are clearly marked. Reykjavík and Akureyri have inexpensive multistorey car parks.

6 Hazards
Roundabouts can be tricky. The inner lane has right of way over the outer; take the outer lane if planning to exit at the next junction. Be cautious when driving past schools and pedestrian crossings. Icelandic drivers do not habitually stop for pedestrians, who are frequently none too cautious in crossing roads.

7 Traffic Signals
Traffic lights follow European convention, with amber for caution, red for stop, red and amber together for stop but prepare to go, and green for go. The word *blindhæð* warns drivers of a blind hill, which can occur on single track roads and demand cautious driving.

8 Gravel Roads
Many of Iceland's rural roads are gravel, narrow and not suited to fast driving. Speed limits are reduced from 90 kmph (56 mph) to 80 kmph (50 mph) on these roads. Drive considerately and use passing places when you meet oncoming traffic. Take care especially where gravel roads meet asphalt and vice versa.

9 Driving in the Highlands
Driving off marked roads is prohibited as it can damage the land and you may be sued for compensation. Many rivers in highland areas are unbridged, so ensure conditions are safe before crossing. Mountain tracks are closed in winter and reopen in early July. Most require a 4WD. Always take a detailed map and GPS.

10 Livestock and Wildlife
There is a lot of unfenced territory in Iceland and it is common to find sheep, horses or cows on roads all over the country. This can be dangerous. Drive carefully as you may be liable to compensation claims if you cause injury or death.

In Iceland, vehicle headlights have to be on at all times, day and night.

Left **The Dubliner pub, Reykjavík,** Right **Whale-watching trip, off Húsavík**

TOP 10 Things to Avoid

1 Pub-Crawling on Payday
Traditionally payday is the day to splash your cash in town on a pub crawl. After the global market crash, the party spirit has diminished, but you can still expect a procession of cars around the city on Friday and Saturday nights, long queues at the bar and a little late night brawling.

2 Fishing Without a Permit
You need a permit to fish in Iceland and will be subject to hefty fines if you do not have one. Fishing season runs June to September and there are restrictions on the length of the fishing season on most rivers. You may not fish for longer than 12 hours a day. Rule violations are taken very seriously.

3 Solo Wilderness Driving
Iceland's habitat can take years to recover from damage, so off-road and solo wilderness driving is frowned upon. Mobile phone coverage in the highlands is not reliable and roads are rarely used. If your vehicle has broken down, stay with it. Always take a map and a GPS device.

4 Speeding on Gravel Roads
The majority of road accidents in Iceland happen where paved roads change to gravel. Gravel roads are common in rural areas and subject to a speed limit (see p122). Drivers should reduce speed before the changeover to gravel to keep control. Loose gravel on road shoulders also causes accidents.

5 Rush Hour in Reykjavík
From 7:45–9am and 4–6:30pm, traffic in Reykjavík can be taxing. Avoid travelling at this time if at all possible; the city's narrow roads are frequently gridlocked. It isn't a big city, but most people have a car and public transport is under-used at the moment.

6 Buying Sealskin
Be careful what you buy in Iceland. Fish skin gloves, wallets and belts are fine, but if you buy anything made of seal-skin and try to take it back, US customs will confiscate it. There are no such restrictions by the UK or European customs departments.

7 Currency Exchange
It has been a terrible couple of years for the Icelandic krona and its exchange rate. It is risky to change money any-where other than the major banks, hotels or bureaux de change, as the currency continues to be in flux and its future is still being debated.

8 Recreational Drugs and Homebrew
Penalties for possession, use and trafficking of drugs are severe, with huge fines and custodial sentences imposed. Alcohol is sold through state-controlled shops (Vínbúðin) and is highly taxed. Homebrew – often called moonshine (landi in Icelandic) – is illegal and can be lethal. It can cause blindness and even death, so it is simply not worth the risk and should be avoided.

9 Sailing in Bad Weather
Ferries will cancel their services in dangerous conditions, but such are the conditions in the north Atlantic that even fair weather sailings can be very uncomfortable for the casual traveller. Seasickness is very common, even on whale watching cruises, let alone longer crossings. Most ferries carry travel sickness remedies.

10 Pickpockets and Bag Snatchers
Crime is rare, but you would be advised to take special care in busy bars and clubs late at night in Reykjavík and around the Hlemmur local bus centre. Keep an extra eye on your belongings and valuables in crowds, on public transport and while queuing at busy tourist attractions.

Left **Main post office, Reykjavík** Centre **Reykjavík Grapevine newspaper** Right **An ATM**

Banking and Communications

Banking Hours
Banks are open Monday to Friday 9:15am–4pm. Outside Reykjavík, the hours may be shorter. There are several banks in downtown Reykjavík, Keflavík airport, Akureyri and in all large towns. Outside major towns you will find ATMs in larger stores, malls and at petrol stations.

Currency Exchange
Banks post legal exchange rates in their branches; you can also use credit and debit cards to withdraw krónur from ATMs but be aware that some bank cards charge extra for currency exchange. Check before travel.

Traveller's Cheques
Traveller's cheques may be used in Iceland but it is nearly a cashless economy, so credit and debit cards are more useful. You can change traveller's cheques at banks, hotels and post offices; pounds sterling, dollars and euros are the recommended currencies. There is no limit to the amount you can bring into the country.

ATMs
ATMs are common. In metropolitan areas they are found outside banks, in larger stores and at some petrol stations. Check with your bank before travel to see if you can use your card abroad and what surcharge will be levied. Cash is useful in more remote rural areas.

Credit Cards
Credit cards are widely accepted. Visa and MasterCard are the main brands used, along with Visa debit cards. American Express is not accepted in some places. Cards are commonly used but some establishments do not allow card use for purchases totalling less than ISK 500.

Post Offices
Post offices are found in most major towns and are open Monday to Friday 8:30am–4:30pm. The main Reykjavík post office is also open 10am–2pm on Saturdays, June to August. Look out for the post horn logo on a red mailbox. International post to Europe takes 3 to 5 days and longer to other areas, while parcels are good value. Stamps are sold at hotels, bookshops and supermarkets throughout Iceland.
🖎 Map L2 • Reykjavík central post office: Íslandspóstur, Pósthússtræti 5, 101 Reykjavík • 580 1000 • www.postur.is

Internet Access
Iceland has one of the world's highest Internet usage. WiFi is available in many cafés and bookshops. The Reykjavík tourist information centre has Internet access (free for Reykjavík card holders) and it is available in many hotels and youth hostels. There are a number of Internet cafés in downtown Reykjavík around Ingólfstorg Square.

Telephones
Note that in the Icelandic phonebook, people are listed in order of first name, not surname. The mobile phone network is reliable along Iceland's coastline but not in the centre of the country. It is a GSM system, compatible with European networks but not US ones. You can hire cell phones. The country code is 354.

Newspapers
Morgunblaðið and DV are the two main newspapers in Iceland, published in Icelandic. You can get English newspapers and magazines in various hotels and bookshops. Iceland Review is a quality monthly English-speaking lifestyle and news magazine worth picking up. Free newspaper Grapevine is a good what's-on guide.

Television
There are three main TV channels in Iceland and much of the content is in English and subtitled. Many hotels have satellite TV and screen major sporting events such as international and Premiership football.

Left **Hot pool, Hveravellir** Right **A 4WD crossing a stream in the Highlands**

TOP 10 Security and Health

Security Tips
Iceland is a safe country to travel in but the usual advice applies. Always lock your car, don't leave valuables on display and don't flash your cash. Keep an eye on your belongings in crowded areas.

Crime
The island has one of the lowest crime rates in the world. However, minor assaults, petty burglary and drug-related crimes do occur, primarily in Reykjavík. The country has a strict gun law.

Police
Iceland's police officers, *lögreglan*, wear black uniforms and police cars are white with blue lettering and blue and red stripes. They carry pepper spray and extendable batons but, with the exception of airport police, no firearms.
◆ *Map M3 • Main police station: Hverfisgata 113 • 444 1000*

Emergency Phone Numbers
The 24-hour emergency services number for fire, ambulance and police is 112. All calls are free of charge. For emergency doctors on call, dial 1770. This links to a medical centre in Kópavogur, a suburb of Reykjavík, for telephone advice, home visits or admissions. For dental emergencies, dial 575 0505.

Crossing Streams
Crossing unbridged streams in the country-side is an art. Never cross a stream in flood and never try to cross just above a waterfall. Use a hiking stick to gauge the depth; anything thigh high or deeper is dangerous. Do not cross a stream by car that you do not think you can walk across.

Coastal Hazards
The coastline and beaches in Iceland are not typically guarded. Beware of incoming tides and estuaries when walking and take local advice. Make sure someone knows where you are. In areas such as the caves at Reynishverfi near Vík, walkers are vulnerable to incoming tides and rockslides, so be careful. ◆ *Icelandic Coastguard • 545 2000 • www.lhg.is*

Sun Care
The sun here is very strong. Do not be fooled by the name! Bring sunglasses, sun cream and a hat, especially if you are walking or planning to spend time outdoors. Windburn is also common and you might want to pack aftersun too – it is expensive in Iceland.

Avalanches, Landslides and Mudslides
Avalanches, landslides and mudslides have claimed many lives in Iceland in recent years. Check the meteorological advice if you are planning to go walking in vulnerable areas such as the Western Fjords, especially during springtime. Avalanche warnings are posted online. Heavy rains can lead to mudslides year-round, so check the weather forecast. ◆ *Recorded weather forecast (in English): 902 0600 • For weather updates check: www.vedur.is*

Healthcare and Prescriptions
You are advised to bring all medications you might need with you. All EU citizens holding an EHIC certificate are eligible for the same level of state healthcare as they receive at home but US and other citizens have to pay. Prescription prices vary and ambulances incur a non-refundable cost. Pharmacies *(apótek)* are often open until late.

Water Quality and Swimming
The water is potable here. Public swimming pools, *sundlaug*, are geothermally heated to a constant temperature of 28°C (83°F). The water is very clean – but not chemically cleaned – and you are required to wash before entering. When bathing in natural pools, check the temperature as it can vary due to seismic shifts and you can get burned.

Above **Perlan dome, Reykjavík**

Budget Tips

1 Online Discounts
Check prices online before buying tickets. From Europe, Skyscanner shows the cheapest day of each month, and the cheapest months when to fly with Iceland Express, who also have regular offers. Icelandair has discounts for short periods advertised on their website. The same applies to Icelandair Hotels and many international chains.
❧ www.skyscanner.net • www.icelandexpress.co.uk • www.icelandair.com • www.icelandairhotels.com

2 Travel Outside Peak Season
The peak season in Iceland is June to August. If you can be flexible with dates, you will find that travel outside these months is much cheaper, with the exception of mid-October in Reykjavík, when the Iceland Airwaves music festival pushes up flight and accommodation rates.

3 The Reykjavík Welcome Card
If you are visiting Reykjavík, make the most of this discount card. It can be bought at the Tourist Information Centre and a number of other locations. It gives you free admission to the thermal pools and museums, unlimited bus travel, free internet access and other reductions. ❧ www.visitreykjavik.is

4 Free Attractions
There are plenty of free things to do in Reykjavík. Visit Perlan (the Pearl); take a free walking tour from the tourist office; visit Hallgrímskirkja or walk down to the beach where the thermal pool is free. The city's art galleries are free and the National Museum of Iceland is free on Wednesdays.
❧ www.freecitytravel.com

5 Transport Tips
Taxis from the airport are significantly more expensive than the airport shuttle. Going via the Blue Lagoon on the way to or from the airport is another way to save money, with Flybus/Reykjavík Excursions from the BSÍ bus station.
❧ www.flybus.is

6 Cheap Stays
Bring a sleeping bag if you want to save money in the summer – many guesthouses have "sleeping bag" places that are cheaper than fully made-up beds. The country's youth hostels are top-notch – you can book private rooms in Reykjavík, and you might have others all to yourself. Or bring a tent.
❧ 553 8110 • info@hostel.is • www.hostel.is

7 Eating Out
Tasty soups in the mid-range or rural restaurants are good value as you usually get free refills. The same goes for coffee. Many restaurants offer children's portions. In bars, local beer is cheaper than imported beer and many have happy hours. You can save money by not buying bottled water as the tap water is quite good.

8 Shopping
Buy local goods as Iceland imports so much from overseas that you won't find bargains on items available back home. If you want to buy Icelandic gifts or oddities, the majority are available cheaper at the airport duty free store. Don't forget to claim tax refunds for items over ISK 4,000.

9 Fishing Discounts
Fishing isn't cheap, particularly if you are caught contravening any of the strict rules. You can buy an Angler's Card which allows access to nearly 30 sites for trout, charr and salmon fishing. Check conditions and timing with the tourist office – the fishing season doesn't run all year round.
❧ www.nat.is

10 Travel Insurance
Check your travel insurance policy carefully beforehand, particularly any exceptions to your policy. The unpredictable weather and adventure sports can cause surprise mishaps. European visitors should carry the EHIC card for any emergency.

Left **Fish Market restaurant, Reykjavík** Right **Campsite at Fjallabak Nature Reserve**

🔟 Accommodation and Dining Tips

Book Early
Book hotels well ahead, particularly during the summer, as popular locations such as Mývatn book up early. Hotels in Iceland's smaller towns and popular domestic holiday spots can fill up quickly, especially if there is an event in town. With often limited accommodation options, it pays to plan ahead.

Shoulder Seasons
Outside the main summer season, prices drop considerably. The shoulder seasons of autumn (September–October) and spring (April–May) bring great savings on hotel rates. Christmas and New Year are usually very pricey. Both these periods can be rainy; weather-wise, late May and early September are great times to visit on a budget.

Package Deals
Iceland Express and Icelandair offer attractive package deals with their flights, often including good hotels at bargain rates plus car hire and tours. Online consolidators such as Lastminute and Opodo also have package deals. Discover The World is the top class package tour operator to Iceland. ⊗ www.icelandair. com • www.icelandexpress. co.uk • www.lastminute. com • www.opodo.com • www.discover-the-world. co.uk

Self-Catering
Groups and families might find that renting self-catering apartments or units with kitchenettes will help their budgets, although be aware that all food is expensive in Iceland. Youth Hostels also offer shared kitchens. Farm stays are a popular choice with families, although you will need to hire a car.

Mountain Huts
Backpackers and walkers can stay in mountain or wilderness huts on established walking trails such as the Landmannalaugar–Þórsmörk forest walk. Book them at least a month or more in advance, via the website below. The alternative, camping in strong winds and horizontal rain, is not much fun. ⊗ The Iceland Touring Association: 568 2533 • www.fi.is

Daily Specials
The cheapest or best value menu in an Icelandic restaurant is usually on the daily specials board or a fixed menu. Local and seasonal food is naturally the best value in any case: think lamb, salmon and seafood. Avoid tourist trap eateries advertising puffin suppers for the best prices.

Fish at Discounts
Seafood dishes tend to be cheaper than the meat dishes in most restaurants, and what's more, the country's fish, fresh from the North Atlantic, has a fantastic reputation. Try cod, haddock, halibut, ray, redfish, herring or lobster. For a quirky snack, *harðfiskur* (dried cod) is available in most corner shops.

Water
In restaurants, there is no need to order bottled mineral water unless you want sparkling water. Tap water is of the same quality as mineral water. If you are walking in Iceland, take a bottle with you and fill up at no cost from the tap or from running streams.

Wine and Beer
House wines bought by the half-bottle or carafe might work out as better value than wine by the glass. Iceland imports all its wine bar one brand, Kvöldsól – made from blueberries, crowberries and rhubarb in Húsavík. The cheapest beer brands are the widely available locally-brewed Viking Gold and Thule Beer.

Cultural Centres
Iceland's museums and cultural centres often have bargain-priced eateries for lunch and coffee breaks – no entry fee required. These include: Reykjavík City Hall, Hveragerði greenhouse centre and Kjarvalstaðir art gallery in Reykjavík.

➜ *Visit www.icelandgourmetguide.com for the best of Iceland's food and drink.*

Left **Interior of Hótel Plaza** Right **Façade of Hótel Reykjavík Centrum**

Hotels in Reykjavík City Centre

1 Reykjavík 101
Close to the capital's main shopping street and National Opera House, this smart place is stark on the outside. Inside, the modern, bright rooms have a contemporary minimalist look complete with wooden flooring, large beds and marble bathrooms. Amenities include a gym and spa.
Map L2 • Hverfisgata 10 • 580 0101 • www.101hotel. is • kkkkk

2 Hótel Holt
Holt's façade has the appeal of 1980s carpark architecture but once through the doors you are in one of the most plush old-style venues in town. It is wood panelled and has its own collection of 19th-century Icelandic artworks and an outstanding restaurant.
Map L3 • Bergstaðastræti 37 • 552 5700 • www. hotelholt.is • kkkk

3 Hótel Borg
Wonderful Art Deco building whose elegance and style is reflected in the immaculate rooms, complete with genuine period furnishings. The décor is black-and-white and floors are marble.
Map L2 • Pósthússtræti 11 • 551 1440 • www. hotelborg.is • kkkkk

4 Hótel Reykjavík Centrum
New hotel in an old building on an ancient site: the timber and red corrugated iron exterior sits above the remains of a 7th-century Viking settlement. Rooms retain their century-old feel but are tastefully modernized. Good service and a renowned restaurant.
Map K2 • Aðalstræti 16 • 514 6000 • www. hotelcentrum.is • kkkkk

5 Hótel Plaza
Light, airy modern building with rooms to match; timber flooring, white walls and furnishings and the suites have views of the older part of the city. A host of good restaurants nearby.
Map K2 • Aðalstræti 4 • 590 1400 • www.plaza.is • kkkkk

6 Hótel Frón
Ninety en suite rooms and self-service apartments with kitchenettes, and the usual services plus WiFi. The efficient, modern Nordic look elsewhere doesn't prepare you for the Mexican-cantina-style bistro and bar. Nice terrace café, too.
Map M3 • Laugarvegur 22A • 511 4666 • www. hotelfron.is • kk

7 Hótel Klöpp
Streamlined place with small rooms and open-plan bathrooms; it is friendly, efficient and located just off bustling Laugarvegur. A sound option for a short stay. Rooms on the upper floors are quieter and some have nice views of the sea.
Map M2 • Klapparstígur 26 • 595 8520 • www. centerhotels.com • kkkkk

8 Hótel Óðinsvé
Excellent value family-owned place that manages to balance the homey 1930s building with modern minimalist chic. Its location off the main streets means less likelihood of being disturbed by rowdy weekend merrymakers. A good restaurant specializing in grills.
Map L3 • Þórsgata 1 • 511 6200 • www. hotelodinsve.is • kkk

9 Hótel Leifur Eiríksson
Across the magnificent Hallgrímskirkja, this small boutique hotel has great views of the church and nearby streets from its upper rooms. You don´t get a huge amount of space, but rooms are tidy and it is unquestionably value for money.
Map M3 • Skólavörðustíg 45 • 562 0800 • www. hotelleifur.is • kk

10 Fosshotel Lind
Reliable hotel with comfortable, barrack-like facilities and helpful staff. There is nothing lacking in the services offered, but the rooms are on the small side and could do with some more features. However, good for a brief stay.
Map N3 • Rauðarástígur 18 • 562 3350 • www. fosshotel.is • kkk

Price Categories

For a standard double room per night (with breakfast if included), taxes and extra charges.

k	under ISK10,000
kk	ISK10,000–20,000
kkk	ISK20,000–30,000
kkkk	ISK30,000–40,000
kkkkk	over ISK40,000

Lobby bar of the Radisson SAS Saga Hótel

🔟 Hotels Around Reykjavík

1 Radisson SAS Saga Hótel

Located close to the city centre, this business and conference venue enjoys views of Rekjavík from all rooms. Master suites are very stylish, with dark wooden floors. All guests have access to the health centre. 🚫 Map J3
• Hagatorg, 107 Reykjavík
• 525 9900 • www.radissonblu.com • kkkk

2 Hilton Reykjavík Nordica

As the name suggests, the décor here is distinctly biased towards monochromatic furnishings and pine flooring. In-room safe, blackout curtains (for the luminous summer nights) and bathroom phones are a nice touch. 🚫 Map Q4
• Suðurlandsbraut 2, 108 Reykjavík • 444 5000
• www.hiltonreykjavik.com
• kkk

3 Grand Hótel Reykjavík

Iceland's largest hotel in an impressive tower block, it has a competent restaurant and a huge spa and fitness centre. Conference rooms make it an ideal business venue. 🚫 Map Q3
• Sigtún 38, 105 Reykjavík
• 514 8000 • www.grand.is
• kkkk

4 Hótel Park Inn Ísland

Large hotel which uses coloured furnishings, breaking away from the spartan palates usually associated with Icelandic accomodation. Its location, close to the Botanical Gardens and free access to Reykjavík's swimming pools, is a bonus. 🚫 Map R4 • Ármúli 9, 108 Reykjavík • 595 7000
• www.parkinn.com • kkk

5 Hótel Cabin

Tidy budget hotel with basic but clean furnishings and relatively compact rooms. Upper floors have ocean views, while some rooms are designed with inward-facing windows for relief during the bright summer nights. Great-value lunch buffet at the restaurant. 🚫 Map N3 • Borgartún 32, 105 Reykjavík • 511 6030
• www.hotelcabin.is • kkk

6 Hótel Björk

A drab exterior but the good-sized rooms with views, friendly staff, decent restaurant and location make this option a firm favourite. 🚫 Map N3 • Brautarholt 22-24, 105 Reykjavík • 511 3777
• www.bjorkhotelreykjavik.com • kkk

7 Youth Hostel Rejkjavik

One of the few Icelandic Youth Hostels with private rooms as well as dormitories, which, along with its location near the Botanical Gardens and Laugardalur swimming pool, make it the best budget option in town. Advance booking is essential. 🚫 Map R3
• Sundlaugarvegur 34, 105 Reykjavík • 553 8110
• www.hostel.is • k

8 Hótel Laxnes

Low-set hotel in a semi-rural location near the former home of novelist Halldór Laxness. Double rooms and apartments with kitchenettes are good, but single rooms echo and are lonely. There is a golf course and pool nearby, with regular shuttle buses into town.
🚫 Map Q5 • Háholt 7, 270 Mosfellsbær • 566 8822
• www.hotellaxnes.is • kk

9 Viking Village

Whole complex built around a Viking theme, with accommodation, restaurants, museum and stage shows. The hotel's exterior is a bit like a warehouse, but the rooms are surprisingly good, with the usual white paint and wooden floors. 🚫 Map P6
• Strandgata 55, 220 Hafnarfjörður • 565 1213
• www.fjorukrain.is • kk

10 Hótel Örkin

Small budget hotel with few frills, run by the Faroese Seamen's Mission. It is well-cared for and it with a friendly atmosphere. Church services are held on Sundays. Price includes breakfast but otherwise you will have to eat out.
🚫 Map P4 • Brautarholt 29, 105 Reykjavík • 568 0777
• www.hotelorkin.is • kkk

Left **Interior of Hótel Búðir, Snæfellsnes Peninsula** Right **Hótel Framtíð, Djúpivogur**

🔟 Hotels Around Iceland

1 Hótel Rangá
Spendid countryside retreat with four-star comforts, especially worthwhile if salmon fishing on the nearby Rangá river appeals. Lodge-style pine cabins and main buildings, excellent restaurant and close to all south Iceland's attractions. ◈ Map C5 • Hótel Rangá, Ringroad, near Hella • 487 5700 • www.hotelranga.is • kkkkk

2 Hótel Búðir
Soulful, atmospheric seaside setting, with only a dark wooden church and the nearby white cone of Snæfellsjökull for company. This old-style hotel (totally rebuilt after a fire in 2001) is one of Iceland's romantic gems. Spoil yourself at the restaurant. ◈ Map A4 • Hótel Búðir, 365 Snæfellsnes • 435 6700 • www.budir.is • kkk

3 Fosshotel Skaftafell
You cannot help but feel that a lot more could have been done with the amazing glacier views, only visible from a few of the rooms. Otherwise a perfectly comfortable base for hiking at nearby Skaftafell National Park. ◈ Map F5 • Freysnes, 785 Öræfi • 478 1945 • www.fosshotel.is • kkk

4 Hótel Klaustur
Strange to find such a large hotel in such a tiny place, though it is well placed for summer excursions to Skaftafell National Park and the Lakagígar craters. Has a decent restaurant and a small geothermal pool next door. ◈ Map E5 • Klausturvegur 6, 880 Kirkjubæyjarklaustur • 444 4000 • www.icelandairhotels.com • kkk

5 Hótel Hamar
Long, low hotel with outdoor hot tubs, top-notch restaurant and an excellent 18-hole golf course. Each room has a large window and door opening directly on to the grounds. Do not miss a visit to the Borgarnes Settlement Centre. ◈ Map B4 • Golfvöllurinn Hamar, 310 Borgarnes • 433 6600 • www.icelandairhotels.com • kkk

6 Hótel Hérað
The institution-like exterior should not deter you as the large rooms are tastefully furnished. The conference facilities are good and helpful staff is a bonus. Restaurant is fine but Café Nielsen up the road is better value. ◈ Map G3 • Miðvangur 5-7, 700 Egilsstaðir • 471 1500 • www.icelandairhotels.com • kkk

7 Hótel Gígur
This well-managed, modern hotel on Mývatn's southern shore, has amazing views of the lake from the dining room. The rooms are a bit small for the price. Watch out for the summer flies outside the lobby. ◈ Map F2 • Skútustaðir, 600 Mývatn • 464 4455 • www.keahotels.is • kkkk

8 Hótel KEA
The flagship of this small north Iceland chain is located in a grand old building in Akureyri. The rooms are well-furnished and quite spacious. The generous buffet breakfast gets a thumbs up. ◈ Map E2 • Hafnarstræti 87-89, 600 Akureyri • 460 2000 • www.keahotels.is • kkkk

9 Hótel Ísafjörður
The solid exterior, providing protection against severe winter storms, hides a warm, comfortable and friendly hotel whose staff go out of their way to help. Rooms are not huge, but have everything you will need for a night or two. Expensive but good restaurant. ◈ Map B2 • Silfurtorg 2, 400 Ísafjörður • 456 4111 • www.hotelisafjordur.is • kk

10 Hótel Framtíð
This delightful old building overlooks Djúpivogur's attractive village harbour and is a good place to rest after a trip to Papey island. Rooms in the main hotel are modern and cosy; also hires out more ordinary wooden cabins and runs a campsite. ◈ Map G4 • Vogaland 4, 765 Djúpivogur • 478 8887 • www.simnet.is/framtid • kk

Price Categories

For a standard double room per night (with breakfast if included), taxes and extra charges.

k	under ISK10,000
kk	ISK10,000–20,000
kkk	ISK20,000–30,000
kkkk	ISK30,000–40,000
kkkkk	over ISK40,000

Above **Gistiheimilið Sunna, Reykjavík**

🔟 Guesthouses

1 Gistiheimilið Baldursbrá

In a residential area close to the bus terminal, this hospitable, cosy place provides spacious rooms with shared bathrooms and family-sized apartments, an outdoor hot-tub, barbeque and sauna. Large breakfast buffet included in the price. ⌖ *Map L4* • *Laufásvegur 41, 101 Reykjavík* • *552 6646* • *baldursbra@centrum.is* • *kk*

2 Guesthouse Anna

Large rooms in a beautiful, comfortable house, fantastic food and a welcoming host. Rooms are *en suite* or with shared bathrooms. It is well-located in a quiet street close to the bus station. ⌖ *Map L4* • *Smáragötu 16, 101 Reykjavík* • *562 1618* • *www. guesthouseanna.is* • *kk*

3 Gistiheimilið Sunna

Smart, hostel-like place close to Hallgrímskirkja. All rooms are clean and functional with access to a kitchenette, and there are either shared or private bathrooms. As is often the case in this late-partying city, noise can be a problem. ⌖ *Map M3* • *Þórsgata 26, 101 Reykjavík* • *511 5570* • *www.sunna.is* • *kk*

4 Hafnarfjörður Guesthouse

This simple, self-catering guesthouse has 2–6 person rooms, shared bathrooms and full kitchen facilities. There is also a dormitory with sleeping-bag accommodation (bring your own or rent linen on-site). Buses to Reykjavík and the international airport stop nearby. ⌖ *Map B5* • *Hjallabraut 51, 220 Hafnarfjörður* • *565 0900* • *www. hafnarfjordurguesthouse.is* • *k*

5 Guesthouse Egilsstaðir

More of a character hotel than a guesthouse, but still with a family-run atmosphere, set in a large renovated farmhouse just outside of town with grand views over the lake. Rooms are all *en suite*; there is a great restaurant here, too. ⌖ *Map G3* • *Off Route 1, Egilsstaðir* • *471 1114* • *www.egilsstadir.com* • *kk*

6 Gistiheimilið-Café Margrét

Through the East Fjords along the coastal road, Café Margrét is a nice spot to pull up for the night, overlooking the bay from the foothills just outside Breiðdalsvík. Four rooms in a chalet, with meals available at the café. ⌖ *Map H4* • *Þverhamar, 760 Breiðdalsvík* • *475 6625* • *cafemargret@ simnet.is* • *kk*

7 Skálhóltsskóli

This accommodation is attached to the cathedral school at historic Skálhólt. Summer concerts at the cathedral (www.sumartonleikar.is) are a bonus. Book in advance. ⌖ *Map C5* • *Skálhólt* • *486 8870* • *www.skalholt.is* • *kk*

8 Gistiheimilið Geysir

Next to the geothermal springs area and a golf course, this self-catering guesthouse has single, double and triple rooms with a large kitchen. Most suited to groups, but can accommodate individual guests; book in advance. ⌖ *Map C5* • *Geysir* • *486 8733* • *www.geysirgolf.is* • *kk*

9 Gistiheimilið Hamar

Seasonal budget wing of Hótel Þórshamar, which also runs another guest-house and a youth hostel. This modern block near the harbour has comfortable rooms; breakfast is available at the main hotel. ⌖ *Map C6* • *Herjólfsgata 4, Heimaey, Vestmannaeyjar* • *481 2900* • *May–Sep* • *www. hotelvestmannaeyjar.is* • *kk*

10 Gistiheimilið Hof

Long, turf-roofed building in a rural location with a sandy beach and romantic seascapes. The guesthouse has 6 self-contained units, with 3 double bedrooms, a bathroom, kitchenette and outdoor hot-tub. ⌖ *Map A4* • *Hofgarðar, 365 Snæfellsbær* • *435 6802* • *www.gistihof.is* • *kk*

Left **Hótel Aldan, Seyðisfjörður** Right **Edda Hótel, Vík**

🔟 Summer Hotels and Eddas

1 Hótel Aldan

Century-old wooden building by the harbour – once a bank – now converted into a 9 bedroom hotel with period furnishings, a bar and an excellent restaurant. More rooms are available in their nearby sister operation, Hótel Snæfell. ✎ *Map H3 • Norðurgata 2, 710 Seyðisfjörður • 472 1277 • www.simnet.is/ aldanhf • kkk*

2 Hótel Stórutjarnir

Conveniently located between Akureyri and Mývatn, this modern lakeside hotel sits in a short, tight valley frequented by geese in summers. Facilities include *en suite* doubles, dormitories, a restaurant and attached thermal pool. ✎ *Map E2 • Stórutjarnir, Route 1 • 444 4890 • 12 Jun–22 Aug • www.hoteledda.is • kk*

3 Hótel Hallormsstaður

Cosy country hotel inside Iceland's most extensive forest, close to Lögurinn lake. The hotel has self-contained wooden cottages, rooms in a large guesthouse and summer-only accommodation with a geothermal pool at the school nearby. ✎ *Map G3 • Hallormsstaður, near Egilsstaðir • 471 2400 • www.hotel701.is • kk*

4 Fosshótel Vatnajökull

Functional, tidy place, with warm but small and simply-furnished rooms that have breakfast included in the price. Given the location, pay extra to get a room with glacier views. Popular stopover for large tour groups. ✎ *Map G5 • Route 1 near Höfn, Hornafjörður • 478 2555 • www.fosshotel.is • kkk*

5 Hólar í Hjaltadal

Site of a historically important cathedral, the island's largest estate and Hólar University, which opens its student accommodation to tourists during the summer months. Call in advance to check room availability and facilities. ✎ *Map D2 • Hólar, near Sauðárkrókur • 849 6348 • Jun-Aug only • booking@holar.is • k*

6 Edda Hótel Skógar

Storm-proof building close to one of Iceland's most impressive waterfalls, the eccentric Skógar Museum and superb hiking trail to Þórsmörk. Plain, serviceable rooms with shared facilities, sleeping-bag space and a restaurant. ✎ *Map D6 • Skógar • 444 4830 • 10 Jun–25 Aug • www.hoteledda.is • k*

7 Edda Hótel Vík

This Edda hotel is classier than most, with *en suite* doubles in the main building and self-contained wooden cabins on the grassy slopes at the rear. Breakfast is served in the lobby; head to Vík for your other meals. ✎ *Map D6 • Route 1, Vík í Mýrdal • 444 4840 • May–Sep • www.hoteledda.is • kk*

8 Edda Hótel Nesjum

Well-placed for glacier trips to Vatnajökull or hiking in the Lónsöræfi Reserve, these school buildings offer straightforward doubles and dorms with shared washrooms and toilets, plus a restaurant known for its evening buffets. ✎ *Map G5 • Höfn • 444 4850 • 10 Jun–20 Aug • www.hoteledda.is • k*

9 Edda Hótel ML Laugarvatn

One of two Eddas in town, this huge complex offers doubles with either *en suite* or shared facilities and an in-house restaurant. It is close to the Golden Circle attractions, a huge pool and Laugarvatn lake. ✎ *Map C5 • Laugarvatn • 444 4810 • www.hoteledda.is • kk*

10 Edda Hótel Ísafjörður

Near Ísafjörður's centre, this school (for most of the year) has good facilities. Rooms have *en suite* or shared bathrooms and sleeping-bag space in the heated sports hall or tent pitches. You will have to eat in town. ✎ *Map B2 • Torfsnes, Ísafjörður • 444 4960 • 14 Jun–20 Aug • www.hoteledda.is • kk*

 Many boarding schools in Iceland operate as hotels during the summer under the Edda Hótel banner.

Price Categories

For a standard double room per night (with breakfast if included), taxes and extra charges.

k	under ISK10,000
kk	ISK10,000–20,000
kkk	ISK20,000–30,000
kkkk	ISK30,000–40,000
kkkkk	over ISK40,000

Above **Reykjavík Campsite**

🔟 Character Stays and Campsites

1 Hótel Laki
Converted farmhouse with smart en suite doubles in the main building and self-contained cabins suited for groups alongside. It is located on the edge of a huge pseudo-crater and lava field stretching north up to Lakagígar. Ⓢ *Map E5* • *Efri Vík, Kirkjubæjarklaustur* • *487 4694* • *www.efrivik.is* • *kk*

2 Hótel Látrabjarg
Originally a boarding school, this cosy hotel has a great location, is close to the beach and bird cliffs. Rooms have en suite or shared facilities. Freshwater trout fishing and horse rental available. Ⓢ *Map A2* • *Near Route 612/615 junction, Patreksfjörður* • *825 0025, 456 1500* • *Mid-May–Sep* • *www. latrabjarg.com* • *kkk*

3 Hótel Anna
Great rural location with the white mass of Eyjafjallajökull rising above. Large beds, low ceilings and old wooden furniture add character to the red-roofed farmhouse. Price includes light breakfast and use of hot-tubs and sauna. Ⓢ *Map D6* • *Moldnúpur, Route 246, between Skógar and Seljalandsfoss* • *487 8950, 899 5955* • *1 Apr–1 Nov* • *www.hotelanna.is* • *kk*

4 Hótel Tindastól
Iceland's oldest hotel, in business since 1884, even hosting Marlene

Dietrich, who was here during World War II to entertain US troops. A fantastic wooden building with a flagstoned outdoor spa and resident ghost adding to the atmosphere. Ⓢ *Map D2* • *Lindargata 3, Sauðárkrókur* • *453 5002* • *www. hoteltindastoll.com* • *kkk*

5 Reykjavík Campsite
The huge grassy slope has room for hundreds of tents, near Laugardalur's swimming pool, stadium and botanical gardens. A 20-minute walk from the city centre, the campsite has a covered cooking area, toilets and showers. Ⓢ *Map R2* • *Sundlaugarvegur 34, 104 Reykjavík* • *568 6944* • *www.reykjavikcampsite.is* • *k*

6 Hótel Dyrhólaey Brekkur
Lakeside farmstead up in the hills above Dyrholaey bird reserve. Clean, warm and comfortable rooms with private bathrooms; some have views of the Mýrdalsjökull icecap. Staff are helpful and the restaurant has a good-value evening buffet. Ⓢ *Map D6* • *Near Vík* • *487 1333* • *www.dyrholaey.is* • *kkk*

7 Hlíð Campsite
Great place to base yourself while at Mývatn; tent pitches have superb views over Reykjahlíð and the lake, with hot showers, toilets and

outdoor sinks for laundry or washing up. Wooden cabins and dorm building available if you do not have a tent. Ⓢ *Map F2* • *Reykjahlíð, Mývatn* • *464 4103* • *www.hlidmyv.is* • *k*

8 Hamrar Campsite
Enormous camping grounds near woodland outside of Akureyri; you do not need to reserve a space in advance. There are toilets, free hot showers, washing machines and tumble dryers on-site, along with a kitchen and covered dining area. Ⓢ *Map E2* • *Kjarnaskógur, Akureyri* • *461 2264* • *www.hamrar.is* • *k*

9 Egilsstaðir Campsite
Scruffy and occasionally boggy camping ground with some sheltered woody patches near Egilsstaðir's tourist information and long-distance bus stop; you need to choose your site carefully. Good shower and toilet facilities and a tiny, sheltered barbeque and seating area. Ⓢ *Map G3* • *Egilsstaðir* • *471 2320* • *www.east.is* • *k*

10 Galtalækur II
Self-contained cabins or campsite near Hekla volcano and Tangavatn lake– you can buy fishing licenses here. Visit the nearby Þjófafoss waterfall. Ⓢ *Map C5* • *Galtalækur II, Route 26, Rangárþing ytra, Hella* • *487 6528* • *galtalaekur2@simnet.is* • *k*

➡ *More farmstays at www.farmholidays.is*

133

General Index

Index

Acknowledgments

The Author
David Leffman is a travel writer and photographer who first visited Iceland in 1981. Apart from *Top 10 Iceland*, he has authored *Eyewitness China* for Dorling Kindersley, along with guidebooks to Iceland, Australia, Indonesia, China and Hong Kong for Rough Guides. He has also led specialist guided tours to China.

Photographer Nigel Hicks
Additional Photography Peter Gathercole, Steve Gorton, Clive Streeter
Contents Outline Michael Kissane
Streetsmart Author (pp118–127) Laura Dixon
Fact Checker and Phrase Book Compiler Bergljót Njóla Jakobsdóttir

At DK INDIA
Managing Editor Aruna Ghose
Editorial Manger Sheeba Bhatnagar
Design Manager Kavita Saha
Project Editor Shikha Kulkarni
Project Designers Namrata Adhwaryu, Shruti Singhi
Assistant Cartographic Manager Suresh Kumar
Cartographer Zafar-ul-Islam Khan
Senior Picture Research Coordinator Taiyaba Khatoon
Picture Researcher Sumita Khatwani
DTP Coordinator Azeem Siddiqui
DTP Designer Rakesh Kumar
Proofreader and Indexer Andy Kulkarni

At DK LONDON
Publisher Douglas Amrine
List Manager Christine Stroyan
Design Manager Mabel Chan
Senior Editor Sadie Smith
Cartographer Stuart James
DTP Operator Jason Little
Production Controller Danielle Smith

Picture Credits
t=top; tc=top centre; tr=top right; cla=centre left above; ca=centre above; cra=centre right above; cl=centre left; c=centre; cr=centre right; clb=centre left below; cb=centre below; crb=centre right below; bl=bottom left; bc=bottom centre; br=bottom right; ftl=far top left; ftr=far top right; fcla=far centre left above; fcra=far centre right above; fcl=far centre left; fcr=far centre right; fclb=far centre left below; fcrb=far centre right below; fbl=far bottom left; fbr=far bottom right.

Every effort has been made to trace the copyright holders, and we apologize in advance for any unintentional omissions. We would be pleased to insert the appropriate acknowledgments in any subsequent edition of this publication.

Photography Permissions
Dorling Kindersley would like to thank the following for their assistance and kind permission to photograph at their establishments:

Þjóðminjasafn Íslands/The National Museum of Iceland; Akranes Museum; B5 Bar, Reykjavík; The Blue Lagoon; Búðir Hótel; Café Paris; The Culture House - National Centre for Cultural Heritage; The Dubliner Pub, Reykavík; Emigration Centre; The Fish Market Restaurant; Fjalakotturinn; Fríða

Acknowledgments

Frænka; Gallery Restaurant, Hótel Gígur; Hótel Holt; Hornið; The Húsavík Whale Museum; Icelandic Fish & Chips; Hótel Ísafjörður; Jarðböðin Nature Baths; Jómfrúin; La Primavera; Osvur Museum; Hótel Plaza; Þrír Frakkar; Radisson SAS Saga Hótel; The Reykjavík Art Museum; The Reykjavík Art Museum Kjarvalsstaðir; Sævar Karl; Settlement Centre; Sigríðustofa; Sigurjón Ólafsson Museum; Skógar Museum; The Visitor Centre's Souvenir shop; Vox Restaurant. Also, all the other churches, museums, hotels, restaurants, shops, galleries and other sights are too numerous to thank individually.

The publisher would like to thank the following individuals, companies, and picture libraries for their kind permission to reproduce their photographs:

4CORNERS IMAGES: SIME/ Giovanni Simeone 28-29

ALAMY: Arctic Images 54br, 65cl, 101cl; Ian Bottle 100tr; Phil Degginger 26cla; Bragi Josefsson 60tr; Juniors Bildarchiv 46tc; Wolfgang Kaehler 68-69; Nordicphotos 98tr; North Wind Picture Archives 30tr; Bjarki Reyr MR 82tr; S.I.N. 55tr; Frantisek Staud 116-117; Haraldur Stefansson 54t, 55tl; Clive Tully 16cb

HÓTEL ALDAN: 132tl

CORBIS: Artic-images 27tl

MARY EVANS PICTURE LIBRARY: 30cl

NATUREPL.COM: Wild Wonders of Europe / O Haarberg 34br

PHOTOLIBRARY: age fotostock/ Jose Fuste Raga 4-5, 84-85; N A Callow 104-105; Imagebroker.net / Christian Handl 11bc, /Dr Torsten Heydenreich 16-17c, 22-23c; Lonely Planet Images/ Grant Dixon 19cb; Nordic Photos/ Inger Helene Boasson 53tl, /Kristjan Maack 48-49, 51cl, /Sigurgeir Sigurjonsson 102tr; Oxford Scientific (OSF)/ Richard Packwood 7tl, 102tl; Photononstop/ Philippe Crochet 28-29

PHOTOSHOT: 19tl; Bryan & Cherry Alexander 94tr

SUNNA GUESTHOUSE: 131tl

All other images are © Dorling Kindersley. For further information see www.dkimages.com

Phrase Book

Icelandic belongs to the Nordic family of languages. Many sounds in Icelandic do not exist in English, so the pronunciations given below are for guidance only. Icelandic has three letters in the alphabet that do not exist in modern English: þ (called "thorn", pronounced th as in "thin"); ð ("eth", pronounced as soft th, as in "the"); æ ("aye", pronounced as i as in "light"). Stress falls on the first syllable of the word.

Guidelines for Pronunciation
Vowels
There are 7 vowels – a, e, i, o, u, y and æ, 5 of which take a stress accent, which changes the pronunciation. The "o" can have an umlaut over it.

a = as in sat
á = ow as in owl
e = as in met
i = as in sit
í = as in feel
o = as in hot
ó = as in hole
ö = "uh" sound
u = as in put
ú = as in fool
ý = ee as in meet
æ = i as in light

Letter combinations
Some combined letters in Icelandic have special pronunciations.
fl = as pl
fn = as p
ll = as in tl
sj = as in sh in fish
ng = as nk at the end of a word and ng in the middle
ey = as a in hail
ei = as a in hail
au = as o in hole

In an Emergency
Help!	Hjálp!	hy-oulp
Call a doctor	Náið lækni	nou-ith ee laek-ni
Call an ambulance	Hringdu í sjúkrabíl	hreen-du ee syoo-kra-beel
Call the police	Hringdu í lögregluna	hreen-du ee leu-rekl-una
Call the fire brigade	Hringdu í slökkviliðið	hreen-du ee sleuk-vi-lith-ith

Communication Essentials
Yes	Já	yow
No	Nei	nay
Please (offering)	Gjörðu svo vel	gyeurth-u svo vel
Thank you	Takk/takk fyrir	takk /takk fir-ir
Excuse me	Afsakið	af-sak-ith
Hello	Halló	hallo
Hello (polite)	Vertu sæl/sæll	vert-u sael(f.)/ saetl (m.)
Goodbye	Bless	bless
Good night	Góða nótt	go-tha nott
morning	Góðan morgunn	go-than morg-un
evening	Gott kvöld	gott kveu-ld

Useful Phrases
How are you?	Hvað segirðu gott?	kvahth say-irth-u gott
Very well, thank you.	Allt gott	alht gott
That's fine.	Það er fínt/	thath er feen-t/ gott
Where is/ are ...?	Hvar er/eru...?	kvar er/eru
How do I get to ...?	Hvernig kemst ég til?	kvern-ig kem-st yieg til
Do you speak English?	Talarðu ensku?	tal-arth-u ensk-u
I don't understand.	Ég skil ekki	yieg skil ekki

Shopping
How much does this cost?	Hvað kostar þetta?	kvath kost-ar thett-a
I would like ...	Ég ætla að fá....	yieg aetla ath fou
Do you take credit cards?	Takið þið kreditkort?	tak-ith thith kre-dit-kort
Do you take traveller's cheques?	Takið þið ferðatékka?	tak-ith thith ferth-a-tiekk-a
What time do you open/	Hvenær opnið þið/lokið þið?	kven-aer oph-nith/lok-ith thith?
this one	þessi hérna	thesi hier-nah
that one	þessi þarna	thesi thar-nah
expensive	dýrt	deer-t
size	stærð	sdaerth

Types of Shops
bakery	bakarí	ba-ka-ree
bank	banki	boun-ki
chemist	apótek	ap-o-tek
fishmonger	fiskibúð	fisk-i-booth
garage (mechanics)	bílaverkstæði	beel-a-verk-staeth-i
market	markaður	mark-ath-ur
post office	pósthús	post-hoos
supermarket	matarverslun	mah-dar-vers-lun
travel agent	ferðaskrifstofa	ferth-a-skrif-sdofa

Sightseeing
art gallery	listagallerí	list-ah-gall-er-ee
bay	flói	flo-i
beach	fjara	fyar-ah
bike	reiðhjól	raith-hyeeol
bus (town)	strætó	straeh-tou
bus (long dist)	rúta	roo-ta
bus station	umferðamiðstöð	um-fertha-mith-steuth
bus ticket	strætó/rútu miði	straeh-tou/ roo-tu mithi
car	bíll	bee-dlh
car rental	bílaleiga	beelah-laig-a
cathedral	dómkirkja	dom-kirk-ya
church	kirkja	kirk-ya
glacier	jökull	yeu-kudl
harbour	höfn	heubn
hot spring	hver	kver
island	eyja	ai-yah
lake	stöðuvatn	steu-thu-vatn
mountain	fjall	fyadlh
museum	safn	sabn
tourist information	upplýsingamiðstöð	uph-lees-eenga-mith-sdeuth
waterfall	foss	foss

Staying in a Hotel

Do you have a table room?	Eigið þið laust herbergi?	**ai**gith thith l**ao**st her-berg-i
double room with double bed	Tveggja manna herbergi með hjónarúmmi	tv**egg**-ya-m**ann**-a her-berg-i meth hy**o**n-ah-r**oo**m-i
twin room	tveggja manna herbergi	tv**egg**-ya m**ann**-a her-berg-i
single room	eins manns herbergi	**ay**ns m**ann**s her-berg-i
room with bath	herbergi með baði	her-berg-i m**eth** b**ath**-i
shower	sturta	st**u**rh-tah
I have a reservation	Ég á pantað	y**ie**g **ou** p**a**nt-ath

Eating Out

Have you got a table?	Eigið þið laust borð?	**ai**gith thith l**ao**st b**o**rth
I'd like to reserve a table	Gæti ég pantað borð?	gy**ae**t-i y**ie**g pant ath b**o**rth
breakfast	morgunmatur	m**o**rg un m**a**t ur
lunch	hádegismatur	h**ou**-deg-is-mat-ur
dinner	kvöldmatur	kv**eu**ld-mat-ur
The bill, please.	Gæti ég fengið reikninginn, takk fyrir inn	gy**ae**t-i y**ie**g feng-ith r**ai**kn-ing-t**a**kk f**i**r-ir
waitress/waiter	þjónn	thy**o**-dn
menu	matseðill	m**ah**t-seth-idl
starter	smáréttur	sm**ou**-riet-ur
first course	forréttur	f**o**r-riet-ur
main course	aðalréttur	**a**thal-riet-ur
dessert	eftirréttur	**e**ft-ir-riet-ur
wine list	vínlisti	v**ee**n-list-i
glass	glas	glas
bottle	flaska	fl**a**sk-a
knife	hnífur	hn**ee**v-ur
fork	gaffall	g**a**ff-adl
spoon	skeið	sk**a**lth

Menu Decoder

bjór	by**o**rh	beer
brauð	br**ao**th	bread
ferskir ávextir	f**e**rsk-ir **ou**-vekst	fresh fruit
fiskur	f**i**sk-ur	fish
franskar kartöflur	fr**a**nsk-ar k**a**rt-eufl-ur	chips
grænmeti	gr**ae**n-met-i	vegetables
grillað	gr**i**ll-ath	grilled
gufusoðið	g**u**-vu-soth-ith	poached
hvítvín	kv**ee**t-veen	white wine
ís	ees	ice cream
kaka/ vínarbrauð	c**a**-ka/v**ee**n-ar-braoth	cake, pastry
kartöflur	k**a**rt-eufl-ur	potatoes
kjöt	kyeut	meat
kjúklingur	ky**oo**-leeng-ur	chicken
lamb	lambh	lamb
laukur	l**ao**k-ur	onions
lax	laks	salmon
mjólk	myolk	milk
nautakjöt	n**ao**-ta-staik	beef
ostur	**o**s-tur	cheese
pipar	ph**i**-par	pepper
pylsa or pulsa	p**i**ls-ah/p**u**l-sah	hotdog
rauðvín	r**ao**th-veen	red wine
rækjur	r**ai**-kyur	prawns
sjávarréttur	sy**ou**-var-r**ie**td-ur	seafood
smjör	smyeurh	butter
soðið	s**o**th-ith	boiled

sódavatn	s**o**-da-vadn	mineral water
sósa	s**o**-sa	sauce
steikt	staikt	fried
súkkulaði	s**oo**k-u-lath-i	chocolate
súpa	s**oo**-ba	soup
svínakjöt	sv**ee**n-a-kyeut	pork
sykur	s**i**k-ur	sugar
te	teh	tea
vatn	vahdn	water
ýsa	**ee**-sa	haddock

Numbers

1	einn	aydn
2	tveir	tvayr
3	þrír	threer
4	fjórir	fy**o**r-ir
5	fimm	fim
6	sex	segs
7	sjö	syeu
8	átta	**ou**tt-a
9	níu	n**ee**-u
10	tíu	t**ee**-u
11	ellefu	**e**dl-ev-u
12	tólf	tolvh
13	þrettán	thr**e**tt-dyoun
14	fjórtán	fy**o**rh-dyoun
15	fimmtán	f**i**m-dyoun
16	sextán	s**e**gs- dyoun
17	sautján	s**ao**-dyoun
18	átján	**ou**t-dyoun
19	nítján	n**ee**-dyoun
20	tuttugu	t**u**tt-ug-u
21	tuttugu og einn	t**u**tt-ug-u og **ay**dn
30	þrjátíu	thry**ou**-tee-u
40	fjörtíu	fy**eu**r-tee-u
50	fimmtíu	f**i**m-tee-u
60	sextíu	s**e**gs-tee-u
70	sjötíu	sy**eu**-tee-u
80	áttatíu	**ou**tt-a-tee-u
90	níutíu	n**ee**-u-tee-u
100	hundrað	h**u**nd-rath
1000	þúsund	th**oo**s-und
1,000,000	miljón	m**i**l-ee-yon

Time

one minute	ein mínúta	**ay**n m**ee**n-oot-a
one hour	ein klukkustund	**ay**n kl**u**k-u-stun-dh
a day	dagur	d**a**g-ur
Monday	mánudagur	m**ou**n-u-dag-ur
Tuesday	þriðjudagur	thr**i**th-yu-dag-ur
Wednesday	miðvikudagur	m**i**th-vik-u-dag-ur
Thursday	fimmtudagur	f**i**mt-u-dag-ur
Friday	föstudagur	f**eu**st-u-dag-ur
Saturday	laugardagur	l**ao**g-ar-dag-ur
Sunday	sunnudagur	s**u**nnu-dag-ur

Useful Signs

campsite	tjaldsvæði	ty**a**ld-svaethi
closed	lokað	l**oh**k-ath
danger	hætta	h**ae**tt-ah
end of bitumen/tarmac	malbik/bundið slitlag endar	mal-bik/b**u**n-dith sl**i**t-lag **e**nd-ar
exit	út/útgangur	**oo**t/**oo**t-goung-ur
entry	inn/inngangur	**i**nn/**i**nn-goung-ur
forbidden	bannað	b**a**nn-ath
gents toilets	karlaklósett	k**a**rl-a-cl**o**-sett
jeep track	jeppaslóð	y**e**pp-ah-sloth
ladies toilets	kvennaklósett	kv**e**nn-a-cl**o**-sett
open	opið	**o**p-ith
parking	bílastæði	b**i**l-a-st**a**eth-i
one-lane bridge	einbreið brú	**ay**n-braith br**oo**
toilet	klósett	cl**o**-sett

Iceland Town Index

Reykjavík Selected Street Index

Index

Discover **traveldk.com**

Explore 1000s of destinations

Create your own guide

Share views with fellow travellers

Receive exclusive offers